A DEVELOPMENTALIST'S GUIDE TO BETTER MENTAL HEALTH

A Developmentalist's Guide to Better Mental Health offers mental health professionals a practical, philosophical, and playful guide to working relationally and developmentally with dilemmas, muddles, and the emotions that accompany them.

The book centers around dozens of letters from writers asking "the developmentalist" for help with a wide range of issues. Organized by topics and themes—including trauma, family and relationship issues, living with uncertainty, workplace problems, and more—the letters and the developmentalist's thoughtful, thought-provoking responses lay out a wide variety of strategies for inviting clients into developmental journeys. When shared with clients, the letters and responses are a rich resource for therapeutic conversations. The book includes theoretical and conceptual background information as well as commentary from mental health professionals who already use the letters and responses in their practice.

A Developmentalist's Guide to Better Mental Health is unlike other practical guides in both its format and its focus on development, especially emotional and social development, as a creative activity.

Lois Holzman, PhD, is co-founder and director of the East Side Institute, the international center for social therapeutics and performance activism.

I0084499

A DEVELOPMENTALIST'S GUIDE TO BETTER MENTAL HEALTH

NAVIGATING EVERYDAY LIFE DILEMMAS

LOIS HOLZMAN

Routledge
Taylor & Francis Group

NEW YORK AND LONDON

Designed cover image: © Getty Images

First published 2026
by Routledge
605 Third Avenue, New York, NY 10158

and by Routledge
4 Park Square, Milton Park, Abingdon, Oxon, OX14 4RN

Routledge is an imprint of the Taylor & Francis Group, an informa business

ISBN: 978-1-032-86625-3 (hbk)
ISBN: 978-1-032-86624-6 (pbk)
ISBN: 978-1-003-52836-4 (ebk)

DOI: 10.4324/9781003528364

Typeset in Galliard
by KnowledgeWorks Global Ltd.

Praise for **A Developmentalist's Guide to Better Mental Health**

"How might we counteract the increasing individualism of psycho-politics? How do we engage the dualisms that split us? How do we develop and perform a greater range of emotional repertoire? Holzman challenges the objective–subjective dualism of the human sciences to help us performatively develop. In her responses to the fifty letters addressed to "The Developmentalist," Holzman illustrates the power of play and gives us a glimpse of the characters we can perform to 'become a head taller'—that is, to become something and someone we weren't. Orienting us to our social-cultural activity of making up the world, she provocatively questions the taken-for-granted ways of our world, shining light on the processual and inviting us to play with what irks and confuses us, makes us feel lost, stuck, sad or hurt, bewilders us, kills us, grinds us down, and much more! A provocative, joyful read for those seeking to develop human consciousness as socio-cultural beings and to find new ways to come together and be together. Enjoy the wonderful journey of curiosity!"

> **Saliha Bava**, PhD, founder of Relational Play Lab and
> professor and director of the Marriage and
> Family Therapy program at Mercy University

"On The Radical Therapist podcast, we explore transformative approaches to therapy, and Lois Holzman's *A Developmentalist's Guide to Better Mental Health* is a perfect fit. This book reimagines life's challenges as opportunities for growth through a relational and developmental lens, offering approaches to break free from binary thinking and create new possibilities. With its engaging 'letters and responses' format, Holzman brings deep philosophical insight into everyday dilemmas, making them accessible for mental health professionals and anyone navigating life's complexities. Rooted in social therapeutics and inspired by Lev Vygotsky, it challenges the status quo of therapy and invites us to co-create new ways of living and relating. This is not just a book—it's an invitation to transform."

> **Chris Hoff**, PhD, LMFT, is the host of The Radical Therapist
> podcast and executive director of the California Family Institute

"Are you struggling with an issue or decision? Do you find yourself in a muddle over something in your daily life? If so, let us introduce you to 'Developmentalist Lois' and her book, *A Developmentalist's Guide to Better Mental Health: Navigating Everyday Life Dilemmas,* in which she shares letters written to her, along with her responses that are filled with ways to get out of the same old day-to-day dilemmas. She joyfully, playfully, and creatively takes readers on a practical and philosophical journey to what could be 'otherwise.' Sorry, but here is a spoiler alert! The aches and pains of daily living can be calls to action. You will be invited to a playground of imagination, to welcome growth by inviting others to join with you and to resist simplistic either/or constructions in favor of building on what we already have. Lois frequently says, 'There's always another thing and another thing and another thing.' Those other things are persistently available possibilities. In a world where we all can feel lost at times, she invites us to 'get lost with others' and recognize our relational existence. Struggling individually can give way to 'How can we go on together?' After reading Lois's book, you will see the value and practicality of approaching our everyday lives collectively and playfully. Seeing ourselves as part of humankind navigating our ways in the world we live in helps us understand our relational importance to each another. A developmentalist approach to life and living stretches from individuals to our collective well-being."

Sally St. George and **Dan Wulff**, professors emeriti
at the Faculty of Social Work, University of Calgary,
and members of the board of directors, Taos Institute

CONTENTS

About the Author

Lois Holzman, PhD, is director of the East Side Institute, the global educational center for social therapeutics and performance activism. With co-founder Fred Newman, she has challenged the epistemological bias of the social sciences, advancing a "non-knowing growing," playful/performatory/philosophical alternative. A transformational change methodologist for decades, Lois supports educators, coaches, therapists, non-profit leaders, community organizers, academics, and others to create performatory environments that build community, activate creativity and hope, and open portals of possibility. In her seminal text with Fred Newman, *The End of Knowing*, and her general audience companion text, *The Overweight Brain: How Our Obsession with Knowing Keeps Us from Getting Smart Enough to Make a Better World*, she introduces a Wittgenstein–Vygotsky synthesis that grassroots activists and scholars alike make use of. Lois is founder and chair of the Performing the World conferences and a chief organizer among the growing performance activism movement. She is the author/co-author/editor of 11 books, including *Lev Vygotsky: Revolutionary Scientist*, *Performing Psychology*, *Unscientific psychology*, and *Vygotsky at Work and Play*, and series editor of Palgrave Studies in Play, Performance, Learning, and Development. She received her PhD in developmental psychology from Columbia University.

ACKNOWLEDGEMENTS

This is the space where the author gets to express appreciation/gratitude/thanks to those who helped/supported/made possible the writing and publication of the book you are about to read. And I will do so. But I first want to turn to another meaning of "acknowledge"—to recognize or accept someone or something.

I acknowledge the historical moment that humanity is living through/creating/adapting to/not adapting to/transforming. I acknowledge the destruction of mind/body/emotion/intellect and of the so-called natural world. I acknowledge the pain and suffering, rage and hopelessness all of us feel some of the time, and far too many all of the time, as we navigate the historical now.

I acknowledge all those around the globe who are doing so many varied things to support others to activate and actualize their caring, courage, and compassion in their own navigation of the now. Their creativity—as "unknown inventors"—generates developmental power. It is to them that I express my greatest gratitude.

And monumental thanks to my letter writers (at the online column "The Developmentalist") who gave me so much to think and rethink through and articulate. Every one of the 50 letters I have chosen for this volume was, for me, a special and specific developmental conversation.

My already substantial appreciation of the talented and dedicated faculty and staff of the East Side Institute increased monumentally during the process of both the column and the book. Their support and appreciation mean the world to me. Thank you also to the practitioners for sharing what the column has meant to them and their life's work. I learned a lot about them and about me from their thoughtful comments. And gratitude to Joan DeCollibus and Shannon Darcy for sharing their images.

I thank my lucky stars to have Janet Wooten, a member of that faculty, in my orbit as both cheerleader and creative advisor. She was the impetus for the column, the book, and beyond.

My thanks to Routledge whose professionalism and support are constant. A special shout out to publisher Lucy Kennedy for suggesting this might be a book Routledge would be interested in, and to publisher Anna Moore for accepting the idea and smoothly steering me through the process.

I am very grateful to the anonymous reviewers of the proposal. The care they took and the enthusiasm they expressed were so very heartening.

I am privileged to live my life with Dan Friedman, my brilliant and funny life partner, and our extraordinary family of choice, human and canine. To them, huge thanks.

And to where I live, in the Montauk land and sea, for helping me zoom out and in.

FOREWORD
A DEVELOPMENTALIST DANCE OF DIFFERENCE

In reading this book, I started to develop as a developmentalist! The writing is engaging, and the narratives in the enquirers' letters are vividly expressed and address many universal concerns: loss, illness, intimate matters to do with family life and rearing children, as well as anxieties about global unrest.

The call and response of the chapters dealing with enquirers' quandaries and challenges provide a stimulating conversational tone to Lois Holzman's developmentalist perspective. Here, she provides an intimate opportunity for readers to learn and observe, as if being present as a third party, to the conversation between the person making the written enquiry and Lois. We listen and learn about the creative options that emerge when difficulties are viewed through the social therapy of Lois Holzman. She invites playfulness with ideas that challenge unhelpful binary distinctions that would restrict a person's options to develop. She is humorous and warmly teasing in some responses and profoundly serious in tone when this seems most appropriate. She raises questions through curious enquiry and avoids the trap of unhelpful "top–down" forms of interaction or instruction. In all, Lois Holzman provides the reader with a direct entry into her social therapeutic practice through her carefully worded and sensitive responses to her enquirers' requests for help.

Lois's practice is full of rich ideas that challenge the impoverishment of individually focused psychology and psychiatry. Instead, she places her practice as a communal, resource-focused, performative endeavour that puts emphasis on the importance of each person as a social being (who is also open and capable of becoming more of themselves).

The later chapters of the book provide useful feedback from participants involved in the correspondence with Lois as well as providing ideas and reflections from counsellors and therapists.

The practical examples illustrated in the body of the book are complemented by a section focusing on the historical context of social therapeutics that provides important core theoretical and philosophical contributions underpinning social therapeutics and a developmentalist orientation to practice. The reader is here introduced to further expositions of social therapeutic projects and provided with helpful links to important reading and online resources.

In this absorbing book, Lois Holzman invites the reader to have the courage to play, to experiment, perform, and take a risk, in ways that could help us all to become more of who we already are. In reading this book, I felt my spirits lift. I am already armed with fresh ideas to take into my practice as a consultant and more of the developmentalist in me than I already imagined.

Jim Wilson

Independent consultant and trainer, UKCP registered systemic therapist; former chair of the Family Institute, Cardiff, Wales, and the Centre for Child Focused Practice, the Institute of Family Therapy London; and author of *The Performance of Practice: Enhancing the Repertoire of Therapy with Children and Families, Creativity in Times of Constraint*, and *Building Creative Relationships with Children and Young People*.

December 2024, Cardiff, Wales

Prologue: How It Started

Dear Reader,

Let me take you back to the genesis of "The Developmentalist" project that rainy post-pandemic night. My thoughts were spiraling—circling a cul-de-sac. My stomach gripped with a low-burn anxiety as I tried to make sense of a TV mini-series I'd watched the night before, called *The Shrink Next Door*. It was a modern-day horror story of a dysfunctional relationship between an abusive psychiatrist, portrayed by Paul Rudd, and his hapless client, played by Will Ferrell. (The series was based on the real-life story of Isaac Herschkopf, MD, whose license to practice psychiatry was revoked by the New York State Department of Health in 2021, after the board's assessment of his professional misconduct.)

As I walked home from work that evening, I wrestled with the gap between what I *believed* about mental illness and psychotherapy (i.e., that therapy clients are *not powerless victims*) and this actual story of victimization and seduction. I put on my headphones and headed home along Central Park West. The cobblestones were slick in the rain. I was stuck. As a creator (and client) of social therapy, my beliefs and values growing out of the radical 1960s and '70s—that is, that therapy clients are not victims to be protected by state regulators who determine and enforce the professional boundaries of therapeutic relationships, but rather that "we the people" can and must create our own boundaries in therapeutic practice—were showing fault lines. What happens when patients and therapists *don't* establish decent and growthful relational boundaries? What if patients *do* need to be protected by the state (although you could argue that New York State did a fairly shoddy job of reigning in Dr. Herschkopf!)? Maybe it *is* wrong for patients and therapists to be friends and colleagues? Maybe "saturated" relationships (à la social constructionist pioneer Kenneth Gergen, 2000) more often than not spawn abuse? Back and forth. Yay or nay. I felt this quandary as a tight knot in my stomach.

I thought of Lois, who has considerable skin in the game on this issue and wondered how she'd navigate this seemingly impossible contradiction. Maybe she could help clear the mental mist. I called her.

For some biographical/historical context, Lois has been an important friend and colleague since the late 1970s when I met her at Columbia University's Teachers College in New York City. I was beginning a graduate program in developmental psychology, the same program through which Lois had carried out her doctoral research on the relationality of early-childhood language development. Now a post-doctoral research fellow at the Rockefeller University across town, Lois would visit us frequently. As we got to know each other, I became interested in the activist work she was involved in outside of academia. I soon joined her and a collective of progressive clinicians, educators, and graduate students who would build the East Side Institute and the empowerment practice of social therapeutics (more, in the pages ahead). Lois and I have been colleagues and friends ever since, and we continue to work and rework the boundaries of our relationship.

Here's an example of a previous quandary I'd brought to her: After I developed atrial fibrillation and was debating a course of action, I talked to her about whether to have a cardiac ablation *or* make tea with Chinese herbs. She helped me set aside my either/or, East v. West thinking and figure out how to creatively use *all of it*—electrophysiology, tea, and more. As a dialectical materialist, she challenged not only the dualisms and dichotomies but an "observer-in-life"/victim-of-society orientation: "Let's *please* relate to ourselves instead as both of-this-world and co-creators of *new worlds*."

Relative to this particular quandary, Lois had been on the front lines with so many other colleagues in the US and worldwide to address encroaching restrictions on alternative therapies. Lois and Fred Newman (the Institute's co-founders) and other lay therapists had come under attack for building (group-based, non-diagnostic) "empowerment" alternatives to the short menu of "pill mills" and seven-minute cognitive behavioral therapy sessions currently available to most working people via commercial health insurance or Medicaid. As lay therapists were being marginalized by new state licensing requirements, Lois was among those whose alternative, community-based practices were dotted across the US. Despite operating in relative obscurity, and without buy-in from insurance providers or professional training programs, these alternative practices were out-performing the clinical status quo. From that practical-critical footing, she addressed delegates at the 2004 meetings of the American Psychological Association, urging them to consider: "Do boundaries inhibit the growth of new psychologies?" (Holzman, 2004). She spoke to the practical achievements of alternative therapies (such as social therapy and other social constructionist, narrativist, and activity theoretic approaches) in which patients and therapists shaped their relationships and responsibly established their own boundaries as they saw fit. "But wait! Had we been all wrong? Look at how 'Paul Rudd' had abused 'Will Ferrell'!"

And so I called Lois with my quandaries and with an idea: There were likely people like me in the throes of either/or, yes/no thinking—wrestling with a dilemma and frustrated with the smudgy, cracked lenses of outmoded or just plain reactionary ways of seeing. What if we invited people to write in with their conundrums, and Lois could respond with advice that might not be recognizable as advice at all? What if she were to create an advice column dedicated to helping people "grow a head taller"—to helping turn people's heads and emotions inside-out and upside-down by inviting new kinds of deliberate, collective activities (new performances) and, thereby, the possibility of growth? The idea of a different kind of advice column was born. She would call it, "The Developmentalist." She told me to go home and write her a letter about "The Shrink Next Door." (You'll see the letter and her response in the pages ahead.) But that raises the question of how come she asked me to write.

Why did Lois think writing was important? Was it to get thoughts and feelings on paper, like journaling? But, it seemed to me, journaling was a relatively private activity of chatting with yourself on your perfect personal wavelength, speaking of yourself, by yourself, and to yourself! Journaling could bring swirling feelings, observations, and dreams into greater consciousness and clarity. But, relative to development, is there more?

I pondered. Maybe the writing-for-help activity was a horse of a different color—a self-conscious reaching out, a smoke signal, emergency flare, a thrashing of the arms directed to *another*—and, through the labor of putting pencil to paper, it invited the aid of the Other and, thereby, created an opening for light, fresh air, and relief.

Writing for help entailed writing *to* and *for* another: Writing *to be understood*; writing to expose (not hide) confusion—that is, *I need you to witness the conundrum. Maybe you can see someplace new to go?* Writing for help could strengthen our "othering" muscles, as we strain to meaningfully connect.

This might be what Lois was getting at when she had explained that writing for help, in and of itself, was half the battle—was growthful. But then she came back with a perplexing caveat: *It's growthful to write for help, whether or not you hit the send button.*

Wait. How could that be? That was so curious. And so, I went back and read what Lois had to say (Holzman, 1997b, 2016; Newman and Holzman, 1993/2013) in her studies of developmental psychologist Lev Vygotsky, who, back in the 1920s, wrote endlessly (and brilliantly) about thinking, writing, languaging, imagining, and how they produced and fed each other. I wanted to see what he had to say that could speak to this curiosity.

Vygotsky believed that, in writing, we do something other than regurgitate our thinking onto paper (or screen). In writing, we *complete our thinking*. Our thinking is born through language. Like an apparition slipping on a linguistic coat, thinking is made visible—it's transformed through language. Thinking and words are melded into something new. And that's just the beginning. Thinking comes into being in writing and then spills into the world—and is amplified and changed and molded and responded to by others. Our writing may look like dried-ink-on-paper/pixel-on-screen, but it's more like song-on-paper—generating more waves of writing–responding–completing–responding–writing that ricochet among us.

Now, here's the clincher: Vygotsky (the dialectician) thought that, while the writing completes our thinking, our writing also *completes us*, the writers. As we write for help, we're reading, pondering, further completing what we write *as we're writing*! It's landing back on us as we write. It's impacting. We respond to what we just tapped out. We are transported and shaped by the words we've spun out of and into the world—and we respond (grow?) intellectually, emotionally, and every which way. Our responses feed more writing. And, like a Himalayan singing bowl, the resonances take us someplace new, *whether we hit the send button or not*.

This is where I've come to in my thinking about Lois's commitment to writing for help. My hope is that, as you plunge into the pages ahead, you too will be inspired by the voices of everyday developmentalists and pick up a pen.

Sincerely yours,
Janet Wootten
New York City

PART ONE

DEAR READER

CHAPTER 1

A GUIDE TO THE GUIDE

By way of introduction, I'm a developmentalist. While I have a PhD in developmental psychology, I identify more with the activity—rather than the study—of human development. I work to support people to develop themselves and their communities. I invite people to see development as a social, creative, lifelong human activity and to practice it in their daily lives. By develop, I mean create new responses to existing situations, transforming what is. These new responses can be feelings, ways of thinking and understanding, ways of seeing and talking, and ways of doing our relationships. Ways of responding to the scariness of the world. Ways of navigating uncertainty and unknowability. Ways of living. Ways of creating new forms of life.

I am a developmentalist because the world—the earth, the sky, the animals, the children, the elders, the families, the villages, the towns, the cities—needs to develop. Without creating escape routes, we remain trapped. Without creating the new out of everything that currently exists, we repeat ourselves. We continue to kill mind, body, and spirit.

Developing (creating the new) is far from easy. The great majority of the world's people are not even aware that developing is possible after childhood, or that development is a social accomplishment, not an individual one. People create it together, rather than it being something that happens to us individually. When the conditions are favorable, this creating of development has no end but is ongoing and continuous. But, when the conditions are unfavorable, development stops.

The idea of doing something new can be daunting, even scary. It is so much easier to stay with what we know, even if that's not working. I am convinced that most of the times we're feeling stuck in our day-to-day lives, we're actually deep in what I call a developmental dilemma—we

DOI: 10.4324/9781003528364-2

need to grow, but don't know it or know how. How we frame the situation and understand the moves we can make and how we talk about the problem to ourselves and with others are limited and limiting. We really need a way to make something new with what we've got, especially when what we've got isn't so hot.

For me and many, many others, writing down what's bothering you can be extremely helpful. This is why I started an online column a few years back called "The Developmentalist"—to invite people to articulate in the written word what's going on with them and ask for my help. I figured if they just did that, if they just wrote it down, they've already done something new with what they have. That's a good first step. I asked them to send me their letters, and I would respond. "The Developmentalist" has become a platform on which I locate the specificity of the life situations they write to me about in the broader cultural context in which our tried-and-true conceptual, emotional, social, relational apparatus has left us isolated, fearful, and stuck. I invite people to interrogate the "thought shapers" that keep us spinning and to consider the possibility of being open to going new places and performing in new ways with others and being more playfully philosophical. I suggest some ways to see and think and relate that they may not have thought of or tried. I give them suggestions for some new ways to perform. I advise them developmentally.

Most of this book (Part Two) consists of a selection of the letters I received and my responses to them. The letter-and-response format highlights the assumptions that keep us stuck and makes concrete the possibilities of seeing, feeling, and relating differently that can emerge. I have come to see the letters and responses as *uncommon dialogues* about common concerns, worries, and existential challenges that produce emotional distress but that often remain in the shadows of both everyday and therapeutic talk. The responses invite the letter writers to reflect philosophically about the day-to-day dilemmas they face (and *how* they face them!) as a means of actively transcending and transforming them. In my experience, this way of engaging with life's social and emotional challenges helps us develop emotionally.

As accessible to non-professional general readers as I hope it will be, *A Developmentalist's Guide to Better Mental Health* is written with therapists, social workers, coaches, counselors, and others practicing in the mental health field in mind. The letter-and-response format highlights a social understanding of emotionality and brings a developmentalist's perspective to the distress, social isolation, and relational dilemmas that lead so many to seek therapy, counseling, or coaching. It invites something other than diagnosing or pathologizing. It offers a practical-philosophical guide for working relationally and developmentally with people's dilemmas and muddles and the emotions that accompany them. Each letter–response pair is meant to model and inspire conversational and relational creativity. As an additional aid, this chapter is followed by a chapter in which coaches, therapists, and counselors share their own responses and discuss how they make use of the letters-and-responses. We also hear back from some of the letter writers who share their responses to my responses.

After zooming in on a developmentalist's practice through the letters-and-responses and commentaries in Part Two, we zoom out again. Part Three situates "The Developmentalist" in the wider context of the global development community it is part of and out of which it grew. It explores how developmentalists have come to understand development in the way that they do, including its intellectual inspirations and its dominant practices of social therapeutics and performance activism. A final chapter discusses materials that have influenced or been created from the basics of a developmentalist's practice.

CHAPTER 2
A DEVELOPMENTALIST'S PRACTICE

As a developmentalist, I invite people to expand their emotional scripts. We humans have created our emotionality. It is, potentially, ever-changing. We can perform new emotions into existence. We can expand our emotional repertoire.

Before proceeding to the letters I received and my responses, I want to share some of what guides how I read and respond—in other words, what being a developmentalist means to me. Each of the sections in this chapter presents an element of the developmentalist conceptual framework: Creating stages, playing, and performing; engaging developmental dilemmas; expanding emotional repertoires; and embracing our relationality.

Creating Stages, Playing, and Performing

A developmentalist's practice is based in a social-cultural, relational, and performative understanding of development. This is different from the common understanding of development that we have been socialized to have. Whether you have studied psychology or not, you most likely picture human development as a series of stages that individuals pass through on their way to becoming adults (think of Freud and Piaget). These stages are believed to emerge in a fixed order owing to maturing of the brain and a reasonable amount of nurturing. In other words, the dominant view is that development is something that happens *to us as individuated selves*. In addition, while, over the past half-century, psychologists have expanded their interest and understanding of development beyond childhood, a stage-like and hierarchical view is still embedded in what has come to be known as lifespan development. This is the case

Figure 2.1 *Theatre Stage created by Joan DeCollibus*

not only for Piaget and Freud but also for other influential psychologists, such as Kohlberg (1973) and his stages of moral development and the hierarchy of needs put forth by Maslow (1958).

A simple way to see the difference between this dominant view and a developmentalist's understanding of development is to picture two kinds of stages (see Figure 2.1).

Stage theories fit well with an image of a ladder with its steps leading progressively upward. My social-cultural, relational, and performative theory fits well with the image of a theatrical stage upon which a cultural activity, a performance, is created and shared. Through this social activity, the actors and crew are building relationships with each other and the audience.

A developmentalist incorporates this theatrical language into their way of seeing human life. I mean this literally. Performing, for me, is more than a metaphor. It's what people do. Creating stages and performing on them are, to me, what people do and how they develop.

Performing in this sense is closely related to playing in the way children do it. This is easiest to see when children are engaging in free and imaginative play with each other, their toys and stuffed animals, and all kinds of objects They create the stage for an elephant and a horse to dance and choreograph their moves, they create a doctor's office and become a doctor for their sick teddy bear, they stage a confrontation between two superheroes, they perform as Mommy making dinner for her babies, and so on. In situations like these, they are being who they are and other than who they are—*at the very same time*. They are themselves, but they are also performing "other."

A century ago, the renowned Russian psychologist Lev Vygotsky identified this kind of play as the leading activity of children's development—in play, he wrote, children perform "a head taller" than they are (Vygotsky, 1978, p. 102). While Vygotsky's insights give us a deeper understanding of what is easily identified as children's play, they do even more—they help us realize that this capacity to perform/to play is the key to *all* human development and learning.

To illustrate, let's look at the development and learning of language, something Vygotsky was very interested in as a cultural-historical phenomenon. He looked at language as a unique form of psychological activity, one in which people not only create words and meanings, but also continuously create new speakers (and signers and writers and readers). Building on this understanding, for decades I have pursued the topic of how humans become what I like to call "languagers" (Holzman, 2018b). I use this term (which I think I made up) to convey more than learning and more than speaking. Languagers create language and use language to create other things—relationships, learnings, material things, and themselves. Languagers are speakers, listeners, conversationalists, readers, writers, poets, singers, creators, makers of meaning. Becoming a languager involves acquiring skills and knowledge. But it's fundamentally a developmental, qualitatively transformative activity of becoming something and someone you weren't.

We can see this beautifully in the process of becoming a speaker when we are very young. I love inviting people to talk with me about this, since most of us have never given it a moment's thought. I especially like bringing this topic to groups of young people in college classrooms and after-school programs. I ask them, "How many of you were once babies?" (They all raise their hands and snicker a bit.) "How many of you learned to talk?" (Ditto.) I go on: "How many spoke English as your first language? Spanish? Korean? Chinese? Bengali?" When I ask how come we all didn't begin speaking the same language, they typically respond that we speak what the people around us speak. We learn the language we hear. I agree and go on to say that, as babies, we're anything but passive in this process, that we play an active role in creating ourselves as speakers. And we do it together with others around us—through playing and performing.

I tell them that each one of us played with sounds and words and sentences as an everyday part of what we were doing with our families, in the house and on the street and playground. Each one of us creatively imitated mothers and fathers and brothers and sisters and grandparents and friends and neighbors and people on television, and *they became part of who we were becoming*, as the unique person that each of us is. Each one of us was related to as a speaker even though we didn't speak a language but merely babbled. It's as if we were in a scene of a play, performing as characters carrying on a conversation. And, even though only one character knows the language, and neither one understands what the other is saying, we're performing that we do. And, through this performance, we transform from babblers to speakers.

I've never spoken with a group that didn't love this conversation. Teenagers tell me that no one ever talked to them about language before and thank me for giving them the opportunity to think and speak about this new thing. College sophomores are intrigued by the idea that learning the subject matter of their courses might have something to do with learning to speak its language.

The fields of psychology, psychiatry, and psychotherapy have done a spectacular job in teaching us and getting us to use their language. This is the case not only for individuated stages of development but for how we name and understand our emotions, our pain and distress, our relationships and interactions—indeed, our lives. From a developmentalist's point of view, this is unfortunate in so many ways. It narrows our view and limits us to what we are told is scientifically proven to exist when, in so many cases, this is not the case. Psychiatric diagnosis is a glaring case in point. Critiques of it abound, not only of its lack of scientific validity and its disregard for the unique experiences of the individual, but also of its authoritarian role in maintaining the status quo of inequity and injustice, its gender, race, and class biases, and its glorification of individualism and suspicious attitude toward collectives and groups. (See Chapter 15 for a description of and references to some of these critiques.)

Psychological language socializes us to understand ourselves and relate to others as isolated individuals who commodify ourselves, who are driven to possess and compete with each other, who see the world in terms of black and white, good and evil, us and them. Many of us feel trapped into certain ways of feeling and relating by this framework and wish there was a way out. For a developmentalist, what is required is to be *other*, so that we can become more and other than who we are. Perhaps individually and as a nation and as humanity, we can become less depressed, less lonely, less angry, and more loving. In keeping with this, a developmentalist's practice invites people to imagine otherwise, to play with known language and ways of seeing in such a way as to see other possibilities and try out other ways of being that give expression to who we are becoming.

Engaging Developmental Dilemmas

This book is written to help you see, reflect, and act upon life's dilemmas. Not the "damned-if-you-do/damned-if-you-don't" scenarios, as we commonly understand them. Not those situations in which we feel forced to choose between two actions, both of which we find unpleasant, distasteful, or downright wrong. As a parent, you want to protect your children as much as you can and think that monitoring their screen time and activity will do this. But you also want to encourage them to think critically and develop responsibility—and to know that you trust and respect them. Do you control them or let them be? Or maybe you had a huge fight with a family member, and neither of you can apologize or forgive each other. But you know that the two of you not talking is painful for the rest of the family. Do you pretend nothing happened for the sake of the family or do you continue to give the cold shoulder? In both examples, whichever way you choose to go, you are likely to have doubts or misgivings.

In a nutshell, that's how dilemmas have come to be understood in our either-or world. Two roads. No way out! We have been raised, taught, and shaped to see and think and feel and experience *dualistically*. Humans are not only bifocal (having both near and distant vision), but we have also become "bipolarized." By that I mean seeing and having to choose either this or that. Near and distant vision is great. "This or that" vision isn't. And so, while we often lament the fact that we are living in a polarized world, I want us to also lament that our eyes have been trained to see polarity. To me, the two seem inextricably bound together. Minimizing or undoing one entails minimizing or undoing the other.

Engaging a life dilemma *developmentally* is something other, something different. It's the activity of viewing the world without our either-or glasses, without feeling that we have no choice but to settle for the lesser of two evils. Engaging life dilemmas developmentally expands our imaginings such that we catch a glimpse of another choice—the choice to grow. Let me explain.

In order to get out from under being trapped, frustrated, and stuck, you need to move out of your usual ways of feeling and seeing and understanding and relating by creatively doing something you don't usually do, by being, if you will, other than "you." We all have the capacity to create new feelings and emotions, new ways of seeing and understanding, and new ways of relating. To keep creating who we are. That is how "other than you" becomes you. With development as the continuous process of creating who we are, we can create new choices besides either this or that. A dilemma engaged developmentally (performing "other") offers you the chance to grapple with *whether and how to keep developing*.

The letters and responses in the subsequent chapters will help you see the difference between dilemmas framed as "either-or" impasses and/or those framed as opportunities for growth. Many letters are from people facing life challenges, people feeling stuck with seemingly bad or impossible choices who are wanting help in how to approach their problems. I respond to how they are telling their story; I wonder how they're understanding their situation and what assumptions they might be making that make them see it the way they do. And I tell them what I see as the particular developmental issue their situation is a part of and how they might need to grow around it—by doing something outside the either-or box in order to see and experience themselves and others in new ways, in order to see and act upon their (hopefully) developmental dilemma. I think of these "conversations" as providing a direction you can take to create a way out of bipolarity and impasse—"a way out of 'No Way!'" In my experience, our lives are enriched, and we all can grow ourselves and our relationships when we see and act upon the developmental dilemmas we face.

Expanding Emotional Repertoires

Growing ourselves and our relationships includes growing emotionally. Growing emotionally means creating new emotions. If development is the lifelong, creative activity of people transforming who they are and what there is into something new, then human emotionality is potentially transformable and expansionary. When we see and relate to emotions as something people create, the possibilities for creating new emotions are endless.

As a developmentalist, I invite people to expand their emotional scripts. We humans have created our emotionality. It is, potentially, ever-changing. We can perform new emotions into existence. We can expand our emotional repertoire.

We are a long way from the days when Paul Ekman and Wallace Friesen (1971) used facial expressions to identify six universal basic emotions. Social scientists have expanded Ekman's list many times over in their attempts to account for and classify the incredible complexity of human emotionality. And, while the majority of researchers and practitioners now recognize the importance of societal and cultural factors in shaping human emotion, "nurture" is still seen as secondary to "nature." And fewer still acknowledge that the very way we conceive of emotions and the language we have come to use to describe them are also major shapers of "how we feel."

How *do* we conceive of emotions? What kind of entities do we take them to be? Would I feel differently if I conceived of my feelings differently? As a developmentalist, I take these questions to be—well, developmental! In my experience, they open us up to possibility. For example, must I name how I feel right now? Are emotions any less social when we "keep them to ourselves"? Is test anxiety the same as climate anxiety? What do we gain and what do we lose by classifying them both as anxiety? Is my anger something inside me? How can I control it? Did my brain/hormones/genes really make me do it? These questions, and dozens more like them, contain many of the assumptions of the dominant individualized and psychologized discourse of emotions that permeates our everyday emotional language. They can serve as invitations to play with this language, to move around and through the tried-and-true and imagine new possibilities.

For too many of us, too much of the time, our all too real emotional pain and distress are depressingly familiar. Like a theatre company that puts up the same handful of plays year after year, we too have a stock repertoire. We lash out in anger when we feel wronged. We feel shame when we experience rejection. We panic when we don't know what to do. We are trapped by our societally shaped, well-practiced emotional life. It is hard to imagine not feeling this way, and so it is hard to imagine doing something different. But we can. We can perform. As one example, we can *intentionally perform* that anger, shame, or panic. I guarantee you will feel different if you do. You will feel something new (and there's no need to name it!), and so will the people you are with, opening up the possibility that, together, you can create something new in your relationship. What happens to the anger, shame, or panic? It is unlikely it will go away, but now it "has company." You have created a new feeling, expanded your emotional repertoire. Performing how you feel, as in the example just given, is just one way to create new emotions. There are many, many others. See if you can find hints to them in the letters and responses that follow in Part Two.

Accepting Our Sociality and Embracing Our Relationality

Finally, we cannot be reminded too often that we humans are social beings. We might feel and even believe that our life activity is a series of encounters with others, our self-contained body-mind constantly bumping into other self-contained body-mind entities. I read that in many of the letters I receive, and it saddens me. But we are not self-contained. We are radically relational. We are born social and we die social. Every step of the way in between is a co-creation with others, past, present, and even future others. Our power lies in embracing this by co-creating some new ways to be together. Inviting people to do that—to take advantage of our relationality—is what ties together the other three elements of a developmentalist's practice.

PART TWO

"DEAR DEVELOPMENTALIST"

CHAPTER 3
AN INVITATION TO WONDER

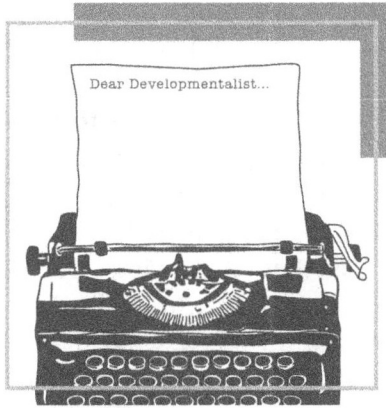

Figure 3.1 *Typewriter created by Shannon Darcy*

Chapters 4–12 consist of 50 of the letters I received and my responses to them. They are grouped roughly according to issues the letter writers have asked for help with. These include family tensions, friendships, workplace challenges, identity and self-doubt, illness, dying and grief, personal loss, as well as strong emotional responses to the uncertainty, violence, and polarization of the current world culture and politics.

My responses invite the letter writers to wonder with me about who they are now and who they might become were they to see through different glasses and think and feel outside the conceptual boxes we have been socialized to live our lives in.

As you read the letters, reflect on your own conversational curiosity. Use my wonderings as a guide of sorts—do you wonder about such

DOI: 10.4324/9781003528364-5

things in your practice? Whether you are a professional in mental health or not, every relationship deserves curiosity, and every conversation invites wondering.

I mostly wonder about people and how we see and feel and think and speak—and that includes how we see and feel and think and speak about seeing, feeling, thinking, and speaking! As much as I can, I invite others to wonder with me. So many assumptions lie within our unexplored ways of going about our lives, ways that have shaped us and too often trap us and keep us locked into non-developmental and even destructive ways of being. When we wonder together, we have the chance to explore how things are, including our ways of understanding them, to play around with our attachments to them, and to discover how they—and we— might be different.

One of the most common "invitations to wonder with me" in my responses to letter writers is about conversations they may or may not be having. As you will read, M. from Chicago ("How do I protect my teens? Should I lay down the law?" p. 36) wrote of not knowing how to protect her kids now that they're growing up. I became curious about how and how much she and her children talked together. I urged her to let them into the conversation she was having with herself. To get her started, I shared many things I was curious about (for example, "How do they feel your relationships are going? Do they tell you when they feel you're treating them like babies and when you're not?"). I invited M. to join my curiosity and, even more, to invite her kids to be curious with her as a valuable way to build their relationship.

Similarly, with A. from South Africa ("I'm overwhelmed with grief over my son's illness," p. 61) who wanted to share her grief, I wondered what her conversations with friends and family members and co-workers are like. I asked her,

> Do you tell them how you feel when they are distant? Do you invite them to share with you how they feel when you tell them both bad news and good news? Do you ask them what they need to be closer to you? And do you ask them for help even when you don't know what you need—inviting them to help you discover what you need?

While the idea of having such conversations can sometimes feel too risky, when people do make that move, they are often surprised at what it opens up for them and their relationships. And people have told me that even just imagining doing it allows them to entertain some new perspectives.

I also wonder with people about many things that seem obvious— for example, about emotions. Centuries of dualistic psychology and philosophy have socialized us to experience emotions as mental states lying inside us and as caused by something or someone. It seems to "go without saying" that, if you're annoyed, like Emilie K. from New Jersey is ("I get annoyed by everyone," p. 23), there must be someone or something that made you feel that way. (Lately, psychologists and many of us call that "being triggered.") But this cause–effect way we relate to actions and feelings, which feels completely natural, is not the way it has to be or even, to me and many others, how it actually is. Causality is cemented into our beings—we see it and feel it everywhere (Holzman, 2018a). We impose it on all kinds of life situations where it's not only unnecessary but distorting. It can lead us down the wrong path, seeking the cause, the trigger, the culprit, the why. Going in that direction keeps us from exploring others, from creating other paths. As I wrote to Emilie K.,

> What if that causal relation, that feeling that it must be the case, is what makes it so hard for you to do something else? What if "getting annoyed" is not an inner state that you either "let out" or try to stifle?

I invited her to step back and see annoyance for the complex human activity that it is, and to investigate it, play with it, and try out new performances of it—and to do all of this with the people that annoy her. A different path? Yes, and one without why.

So many other couplings, not only of actions and feelings but also of one action with another or one feeling with another, stem from this meta-coupling of cause and effect. I address several of them in my responses to letters. For Sue from New Jersey ("What if I can't just forgive and forget? p. 31), forgiveness is required to move on with her family. She can't forgive and so she is stuck. In "I've been traumatized … but then, who hasn't?" p. 25). Confused and Traumatized is grappling with trauma, in both her personal history and our culture's obsession with it. Her specific coupling is of trauma and suffering. I invite her to explore this relationship and discover if it's as tight a marriage as it seems.

I wonder, can one suffer without trauma? Can one experience trauma without suffering?

A large part of a developmentalist's practice is inviting people to wonder about the ramifications of identifying things in a particular way (for example, calling other people the causes of how we feel), how we connect them with other things (for example, forgiving and letting go), and how else we might identify them. For better or worse, people feel differently about their or a family member's difficulty sitting still and staying focused, depending on whether that is related to as a disorder of an individual brain, some feature of the culture and social environment that is at odds with who and how the person is, or something else entirely. Calling it ADHD is very different from identifying it as restlessness, boredom, or lack of concentration, and the ramifications are huge.

To uncover the assumptions embedded in our language is to begin the developmental process of getting unstuck. The 20th-century philosopher Ludwig Wittgenstein, who is one of my heroes, called it clearing "the mental mist ... that enshrouds our ordinary use of language" (Wittgenstein, 1965, p. 17). He was keenly sensitive to and greatly pained by the ways that our ways of speaking and thinking so often get us into intellectual and emotional muddles, confusions, traps, narrow spaces, tormenting and bewildering us and giving us mental cramps.

Speaking of traps leads us to the either-or dilemmas people often find themselves facing, which is a common theme among the letter writers. We are socialized to see our choices as limited to two, as writers Pandora's Box ("I don't want my kids living on screens!" p. 34)," and S.F. ("Is it time to retire from the company I founded?" p. 73) did. Given the polarized world we must navigate, it is no surprise our vision is limited in this way. I invite people to take off those bipolarized glasses for a moment and see what else there is to see.

This isn't easy; it's often just a blur at first, but, if you work at it, actively and imaginatively, you are likely to see other options for what you could do. In addition to this or that, it turns out there's always *another thing* and *another thing* and *another thing*. What was an either-or dilemma is transformed into a developmental dilemma. Whether and how you act on it have to do with choosing to grow.

Chapter 4
Trapped by Language/Psychology-Speak

I'm Triggered by Trigger Talk

Dear Lois,

The word "trigger" triggers me into being a person with little compassion for those among us who will not, or who are unable to, *own* their issues. To me, to say one is "triggered" by one thing or another seems to be a shirking of personal responsibility. Why point the blame and make everything about how you were "triggered" when something is not going the way you want?

For example, a friend says to me: "I am triggered by my mother's critical comments about how I live my life. I cannot converse with my mom, because she triggers me." I want to say to them: "Hey, you *know* your mother's criticisms of you are endless. So when you talk to her—*if* you talk to her—stay away from discussing your life and your life decisions that are going to draw fire. Talk to her about the weather! But stop looking for approval. *Own* your life; *own* your decisions."

Help me figure out what to do with my lack of compassion when I hear the words, "that triggers me."

Wondering in Massachusetts

Dear Wondering,

I welcome your letter, as I always appreciate those who take the time to write to me. Sharing your "issue"—being triggered by those who say they are triggered—allows me to invite you to go in many directions with me. One obvious one is, how come you chose

DOI: 10.4324/9781003528364-6

to describe yourself as triggered? A joke, perhaps? Even so, it does put you in the category of people you have no compassion for! Perhaps worth exploring.

Another direction to go is what people mean when they say they are being triggered. Does everyone mean the same thing? Your interpretation is that such people are shirking responsibility for their lives. *All of them? Really?*

"Trigger" used to simply mean "catalyst." Then, it entered the psychological field in relation to what's now called PTSD (post-traumatic stress disorder), to refer to a situation when a sound or smell or other stimulus acts like a sensory reminder of something traumatic (like fireworks might for someone who was in combat) and a "re-lived memory" and/or inappropriate reaction to what's happening now.

And then, around the turn of this century, people greatly broadened the meaning of "trigger" to all kinds of situations where they are upset, disgusted, or angry. And it's now one of those buzz words, like "addicted" or "traumatized"—that some people (like you) find terribly annoying, and others find extremely helpful. I suggest you not assume or interpret but engage in conversation with those who say they are triggered. How else might they characterize feeling upset, scared, morally outraged? What do other people in their lives say when they feel these ways? What would you say if you didn't say triggered?

Develop your curiosity muscles! Both about people and about buzz words.

And then there's compassion and its lack. You want help to figure out what to do with your lack of compassion for people who say they're triggered. That one's easy! Forget about it! It's not a problem.

You don't need compassion to be curious. In fact, creating a conversation in which everyone is being curious with and about each other might produce some collective compassion. And what a beautiful thing that could be!

Developmentally yours,
Lois

Everyone Annoys Me!

Dear Developmentalist,

I'm writing to ask for help to develop around Getting Annoyed!

I am easily, intensely and very often annoyed by the actions, words or seeming inabilities of others—and really often it's by people I most care for! I am noticing increasing annoyance and want to do something else. I hope you can help!

I can't believe how annoyed I get—all the time! I must think I know it all better! It's not giving or friendly. I'm unhappy, bored and burdened with getting annoyed by my friends and loved ones, not to mention people I work with. I mean, I MUST annoy them, too. I've got to think that I'm pushing people away.

Telling myself not to get annoyed isn't working at all, by the way. Looking forward to your thoughts, and your development guidance!

Regards,
Emilie in New Jersey

Dear Emilie,

What is it to be annoyed? Let's investigate!

I love your invitation because it's not only you who gets annoyed. We all do. And my guess is that 99% of us wish we did it a lot less. I think it might help us get there—or at least closer—if we had a sense of what we're doing when we "get annoyed."

Like most people, you probably think that your annoyance is caused by the actions of others, that what they do or don't do, or how they do it or don't do it, causes you to "get annoyed." I'll challenge that causal connection in a little bit, but for now, let's unpack what "getting annoyed" feels like for you.

When they annoy you, do your friends and loved ones irritate you? Upset you? Disappoint you? Frustrate you? Shock you? Anger you? Do you feel sad? Afraid? Stuck? I wonder about that and invite you to join me. Because our emotionality is very complex and messy and smushed together—we rarely (if ever) are feeling only one thing at a time. I invite you to explore the messiness of your emotionality, especially when you "get annoyed." You might surprise yourself and discover that "annoyance" is the least of it!

My invitation to ponder these questions in relation to how you are living your life, emotionally-socially speaking, comes from how you opened your letter, when you wrote: "I am easily, intensely and very often annoyed by the actions, words or seeming inabilities of others and really often by people I most care for." It's the "by" in that sentence that's troublesome, not abstractly, but in living our lives. For, there must be a cause of the annoyance, right? There I am, happily cooking dinner, engrossed in a good book, walking to work, having a glass of wine with friends, and such and such happens, and suddenly I am so annoyed! Something must have caused it, and it feels like the cause of my annoyance is what just happened, what so-and-so did or didn't say or do. This seems natural, given that we're told so often that we can be "triggered," and that someone "made me feel or do something" that seeing it that way feels "right" to us.

But what if it's that connection, that causal relation, that feeling that it must be the case, that makes it so hard for you to "do something else"? What if "getting annoyed" is not an inner state that you either "let out" or try to stifle? You say that isn't working, and I'm not surprised.

Such a complex human activity as annoyance (both getting annoyed and being annoying) deserves a lot more work. Like investigating. And playing with. And trying out new performances of. And creating meaning with. Most importantly, all this is best done with the people who annoy you!

Let me know how it goes!
Developmentally Yours,
Lois

I've Been Traumatized … But Then, Who Hasn't?!

Dear Developmentalist,

I've been thinking about trauma, grief and healing, especially after the latest mass shootings in the US. I believe that trauma is an ordinary part of human life—it's everywhere—beginning with the trauma of birth.

I am also intrigued by the etymology of the word trauma: "physical wound"; a Latin medical term, from the Greek trauma "a wound, a hurt; a defeat." And I also see how we live in a culture that has become obsessed with trauma.

I had traumatic experiences as a child, having been exposed to sexual matters at way too young an age. My parents were neglectful, and then there were the ordinary kinds of abuse most women experience, some more traumatic than others. I have been doing therapeutic work to "heal these wounds."

On the same day as my partner tested positive for Covid, I found out that a friend I've known all my life committed suicide. Four days later, I came down with a wicked case of Covid. I spent 24 hours sobbing off-and-on, feeling sick and filled with anger and grief: I was in pain! I had an intense and horrible dream about my rage towards my mother. I obsessed over negative thoughts until I felt despair. I was enraged at myself for getting sick and at the world for being so violent and unjust. Clearly, I was dealing with the grief of losing a dear friend to suicide. I was spinning out of control emotionally, as if I had become the little girl who couldn't be loved, cared for and comforted. Even with vaccines, my Covid seemed worse than everyone else's. It was as if the virus were moving some of the emotional trauma out of my body. Was I working out something that needed to get resolved? I want to say it has been a bit … traumatic!

I read your posts about language games, and I'm intrigued by the trauma/healing/grief language game. Is it developmental to use the same language to talk about healing from physical wounds and sickness as it is to heal from emotional wounds? Is there a developmental way to understand trauma?

Sincerely,
Confused and Traumatized

Dear Confused and Traumatized,

I am so sorry that you've been having such a hard time with so much going one that's both physically and emotionally painful. It sounds truly awful. It also sounds like you've gone through this painful period and are now reflecting on how we speak about and understand such experiences. I'm glad you're "intrigued by the trauma/healing/grief language game"—exploring it can be a very emotionally developmental activity!

You mention that our culture has become obsessed with trauma, and I agree. Lots of people agree, and some are talking about it, like the writer at Vox for whom it's become the "word of the decade" or the NYTimes op-ed writer, who wonders, "If everything is trauma, is anything?" I, too, wonder.

When a culture becomes obsessed in this way, that is, by the expansion of particular words and concepts—which have been created in particular and relatively narrow contexts—into an ever-widening swath of everyday experiences, we lose so much. We lose ourselves in the swarm of buzz words. We lose what was our ordinary language. We lose our imagination to create our own new expressions. We lose our wholeness. We lose the political, social, and cultural world.

But so many people are helped by the language of trauma that I would be remiss if I just left you with all this loss! People say that trauma gives them a new understanding of themselves, clarity, closure, healing, and much more. I certainly acknowledge that, and I'm very glad for their relief.

The losses, it seems to me, stem from how today's trauma has come to frame human experience. Trauma is used so broadly and widely—sometimes as an event, sometimes as its aftermath, sometimes as an explanation—that it can feel at times that trauma is all there is and all that we are. In a park near my house there is a stone wall with these words from Gertrude Stein etched in it: "I am, because my little dog loves me." Taking great, non-poetic, license with Gertrude, our culture increasingly pressures us to say, "I am, because I've been traumatized."

Can we be in pain without having been traumatized? Can we suffer without trauma? I have been known to ponder such questions. You seem ready, Confused and Traumatized, to join me. I hope so.

Another thing about today's trauma is that it's seen as living inside an individual person, physically and psychologically, which makes a lot of human atrocity hard to see and deal with socially, culturally, and politically. Murder is an act of violence. Rape is an act of violence. Are they more or less so by virtue of being identified as traumatic? The poverty of the world is indefensible cruelty, whether or not anyone—or everyone—is traumatized by it. I don't want the horrific things human beings do to one another to take a back seat to trauma. They are horrific enough.

As to your questions, here's my thinking. "Is it developmental to use the same language to talk about healing from physical wounds as it is to heal from emotional wounds?" Developmental or not, people do do it—a lot! The developmental question is: What is that way of speaking doing with, to, and for us? You then ask, "Is there a developmental way to understand trauma?" If it's done exploratorily, like the conversation you and I are having here, then I think it just might be. (By the way, I think you would have answered the same way I just did.)

Developmentally yours,
Lois

That Explains It: Her Ex-Boyfriend Is Unhinged

Hi Lois,

Recently I stumbled upon an email, mistakenly sent to a larger group of friends, and saw a conversation about one of our friends who was "becoming unhinged" in the course of a painful break-up. There was a link to a government website describing the official diagnosis and tips for living with someone who has his "condition," lending further authority to the diagnostic label. Applying a diagnosis in these situations, one friend offered, was a way to make it hurt less, for all of us.

There were no trained professionals on this email chain, yet I was astounded by the confidence with which they seemed to share in applying a psychological diagnosis. I was reminded how ingrained the language of psychology is in our world, and how psychology is used to help deal with life's bitter blows—in this case, to help a friend understand and create distance from the ex-boyfriend, to boost her self-esteem, and speed recovery.

I was saddened at how invoking a psychological diagnosis (behind the boyfriend's back) became a wedge and a wielding of psychology to establish superiority, a moral high ground, and so maybe hurt less. It seems that people use diagnoses—both applied to others and to themselves—to help them feel better when things are awkward, painful or when life doesn't go as they wanted it to go.

My question has to do with wondering how it is that people find diagnosis helpful? Is there room for "diagnosis light" (pop-psychology style) that explains in shorthand how the situation is not unique to you—without engaging the indelible and often damning effects of an MD's or PhD's diagnosis?

Signed,
Eavesdropping on a drama

Dear Eavesdropping ...,

Thanks for your question and its backstory. I find it a juicy one! It invites us to perform philosophically for a little while—to explore assumptions underlying diagnosis as a "knowing" activity, and to play a bit with varieties of diagnostic languaging.

Your story illustrates one of the many ways that people can find a diagnosis of a mental disorder helpful, regardless of the harm it might do to themselves and/or others. In your story, it's not the person diagnosed who feels better; it's his former girlfriend whose use of a psychological diagnosis was "a wedge and a wielding of psychology to establish superiority, a moral high ground, and so maybe hurt less."

Psychiatric diagnoses claim to identify a cause and give an explanation: "What a relief! Now I know WHY (this happened, he did this, I feel this way, etc.)." We've been socialized to believe in causes, not just for apples falling from trees, but for every kind of human feeling, thought, action, and interaction. So, better to live with the false belief that now you know what's wrong—there's an explanation for your or someone else's actions and/or personality; there's a cause for the pain you're experiencing and causing others to experience—than to deal with all the messiness of what it means to live and love.

I'm a passionate advocate for exploring all our assumptions, and exploring causality is way up there at the top of the list. It can be eye-opening and transformative to see how obsessed we are with cause in everyday life and how that can limit possibilities. If we're more concerned to identify the cause of something—say, why a friend snubbed you, or why you yelled at your teenage son—than with ways to move on with your relationships and your life, we cut ourselves off from creating with whatever emotions we might be experiencing; we cut ourselves off from developing.

You ask, "Is there room for psychological diagnosis light, pop-psychology style?" My response is *yes, yes, yes*—if it's done in a playroom. A playroom can be anywhere; it's not a special place, but an environment people create together. To play the diagnosis game in such a playroom is to play with words and concepts and conversations and thoughts and feelings—how have we come to speak/write/think this way; is "your way" the same as "my way"; what if we make a "new way"? And, then, do that over and over and over again. Unless we approach diagnoses as things to play with, they can, and too often do, become "truths"—that explain and constrain and control our lives.

Developmentally yours,
Lois

CHAPTER 5
FAMILY LIFE

What if I Can't Just Forgive and Forget?

Dear Lois,

I love "The Developmentalist." The letters give me new ways to think/ do/perform. I'd love to hear your thoughts on forgiveness, compassion and letting go of hurts.

My sister and brother were hurtful and attacking during a period (2.5 years ago) when my mother was dying. On one hand, I understand this came out of their own pain and that I should be compassionate. On the other hand, it was very hurtful and malicious.

While I have told my sister that I'm not interested in a relationship with her, I go to major family events (weddings, bar mitzvahs) about once a year.

I have made progress over the past two years, but I haven't been able to forgive. And, I find it challenging to let it go fully. I can't decide if the best thing would be to just completely stop relating to all of them. Can you give me performance tips? … a new way to see?

Sue, New Jersey

Dear Sue,

Thank you so much for your enthusiasm for "The Developmentalist"! I'm so happy that it gives you new ways to be/become.

And thank you for inviting me to respond to the topic you offer, and to what in your life is prompting your own thinking

DOI: 10.4324/9781003528364-7

about this. I think it will resonate with readers, as most of us have been hurt by family members and those we're close to at some time in our lives.

What do we do now? How do we deal with and relate to what has happened?

For some of us, the incident and the hurt become the defining feature of the relationship we have had. It seems from what you say that this is the case for you and your siblings. Some people stop speaking to each other. Others try to mend the rift. Some succeed and some fail.

While you have stopped speaking to your sister, it's hard to tell where you are on this. I wonder if you have tried to mend the rift but failed. Have you told your sister and brother how you feel and what you want? Was their attack on you out of character for them? I also wonder how other family members and friends think about the situation and how they relate to how you are with your sister. If your answers are "No" and "I don't know" you should consider asking them.

As for "forgiveness, compassion and letting go of hurts"— are they connected for you? If they are, it's worth exploring how that connection might impact how you're feeling and dealing with the painful situation you're in. However else they might be connected (and I do hope you explore this), they sound an awful lot to me like "shoulds"—ways you think you should feel and act. It must be a burden to carry these around all the time.

But why should you? Seriously. Do you have to forgive (what does that even mean?) your sister and brother in order to see them as human beings in your life, as two people you grew up with, who loved your mother?

I don't believe you have to forgive people in order to "go on" with them. More than once, I have felt wronged and attacked and hurt. I don't think I've ever forgiven the people for what they did, but that hasn't overdetermined how I feel toward or relate to them. Your sister was your sister before she and your brother were hurtful and attacking 2.5 years ago—and she still is. Forgiveness isn't a condition for an active, even an intimate, relationship. If it was, nobody would talk to anyone!

My thoughts on "letting go of hurt" are similar. You don't have to. What would be helpful and growthful is for you to make the hurt "the size" it deserves to be in your whole life—who you are and are becoming. It's not the totality of YOU.

You asked me for performance tips. Sue, I have just one: Lay down your burden.

Developmentally yours,
Lois

I Don't Want My Kids Living on Screens!

Dear Lois,

I have two kids, 9 and 12, and am concerned that though my husband and I have tried to protect them from the craziness of the internet and social media, we haven't done enough. Now they're constantly on their screens.

We took a middle road as did many parents we know. We gave our kids phones and iPads, but also set up child safety filters. We even got two WIFI accounts, so that we could turn off the WIFI in the kids' bedrooms. We try to limit their screen time, but that's next to impossible.

I already see how our daughter is being hurt. Last week, she posted about volunteering to pick-up trash on the beach and got 2 likes, while another girl in her class posted a picture of herself wearing a bikini top and got 200 likes. She was devastated.

I feel like we've opened Pandora's box by giving them this technology. Now we are scared that we may have done the wrong thing, or not enough. Could we have stunted their development by being too permissive? I don't want my kids living in a crazy virtual world. That future is scary.

But all this is me being emotional. Is there any way to be more rational about this?

Sincerely,
Pandora's Box

Dear Pandora's Box,

I'm so glad you wrote me! It gives me a chance to share some of my thoughts on "children and screens." That shorthand is the name of a very useful resource that you and other parents should get to know. Hosted by the Institute of Digital Media and Child Development, it's filled with the latest research, events to attend and parenting tips.

Which is evidently very needed these days. The fears and uncertainty you shared about children's and teens' use of smart phones and social media overall echo those of millions of parents in nations of the world with wide-ranging and affordable Internet access. (It's a different story for poor countries ...). Wanting to protect your children from danger is part of what it means to be a parent. And so is wanting them to develop good sense and responsibility. As you well know, there's no blueprint for either (although there's no shortage of manuals claiming to show you the right way.)

The question is, what's the right way for *your* family? And that begs a bigger question—What kind of family do you, your 9-year-old, your 12-year-old, and your husband want? What kind of relationships do you want to have with each other? Do any of you want to push the social and cultural norms of what a mother should be, what a father should be, how children should act, how siblings should relate? And, if so, how? And how far? Have you all ever talked with each other about any of this? I recommend you do—over and over again—because the circumstances in which you all are living together are continuously changing.

As caring, responsible parents, I'm sure you and your husband talk with your children about social media. I wish I knew how those conversations went—are they more "rule talk" than genuine conversations? I wonder how creative and intimate they've been. For example,

> What was the conversation like before you got them their phones and iPads? (Did everyone share excitement, worry?)
> What was it like when you gave them their phones? (Did you tinker with them together?)
> What was it like when they started learning how to use their phones? (Did you all do "show and tell" time?)

Have you been involved as they continue to use their devices? (Have you shared some of the new things you're discovering as well as trying out some of what they're discovering?)

You say you're being (too) emotional and want me to help you be more rational. Sorry, but I can't help you with that, as I believe rationality is not the way to go. I can, however, help you be more relational—to create space for family sharing and discovery about social media (the good and the bad) in *our* world.

Turns out (according to Wikipedia), there was something else locked in Pandora's box when everything else (the ills and evils) came out—and it's evidently still there. Know what it is? Hope. Perhaps your family can turn your angst (and whatever your children are feeling) into a developmental experience for all—and free the hope.

Developmentally yours,
Lois

How Do I Protect My Teens? Should I Lay Down the Law?

Dear Lois,

I have two kids in their teens. They're very mature in some ways—and I think actually good and responsible kids—but sometimes they do stupid or potentially dangerous things that make me want to lay down the law. I feel that I have a responsibility as their mother to not let them get hurt—either physically or emotionally—so when they hang out with friends who seem too rough or too mean or maybe into drugs or alcohol, I feel my antenna go up. I want to protect them from getting influenced or being led into situations where they could get really hurt. But at the same time, I want to keep building a trusting relationship with them where they can feel free to come to me to talk about what's going on in their lives. I could use some help with this conundrum of constantly fighting the pull to relate to them as children (i.e., "my babies") when I honestly don't want to. This can't be good for any of us, but I can't seem to stop.

M.D., Chicago

Dear M.D.,

Thanks so much for your letter. The specific issue you want help with points to one of the great challenges of parenting. As I see it, that challenge is to create environments for the ongoing growth of trusting and positive relationships even as you and your children are continuously changing! It's hard to focus on creating the relationship when you hardly recognize who your eight-year-old has become by age sixteen.

Perhaps a way out of your conundrum is to relate to it—you guessed it!—relationally. Not as a pull you have to fight against, not as an either-or choice you have to make to protect your children or build a trusting relationship with them. Not as a problem that you have to solve. But as a time in your life as a family when you have the opportunity to create how you will go on together.

I want you to mull that over for a while—how you will go on together. It's such a different question from "What should I do?" More than a different question, it's a different kind of question. It's a developmental question. A social question. A relational question. A creative question. A how question.

We don't pay enough attention to how we do things. We get caught in the what. Like you asking yourself, Should I keep quiet when I have a bad feeling about someone they're hanging out with? Should I set ground rules on what they can do and not do? Should I protect them or not? Am I building a trusting relationship or not?

The decision is not to do one or the other. The issue is how do you do both.

And, M.D., you've done this before. You have experience doing both. When your kids were little and they crawled to electrical outlets, touched the stove, pulled the cat's tail, hit or bit another child, cried when their brother was mean, you covered the outlets, said no, scolded, talked to and comforted them. You didn't "lay down the law" but you did what you felt you needed to do to protect them from being harmed and harming others, both physically and emotionally. And you did these things without qualms or worries that you weren't building a trusting relationship with them. You were protecting them *and* building a loving, trusting relationship!

How to do this now that they're teenagers is not something you can discover on your own. You have to open up the conversation you're having with yourself. You have to include your kids in it. To help you, here's some things I'm curious about. I invite you to be curious about them too. Even better, inviting your kids to be curious with you will be invaluable for creating how you will go on together.

How do they feel your relationships are going? Do they tell you when they feel you're treating them like babies and when you're not? I bet the difference is in how you do it, not what you do. Have you talked with them about this conundrum of yours? What do they think of it? How do they experience it? Do they have any ideas of what you can do or what together you can do? Do you ask them to tell you about their friends, what they like about them and being with them? Are they aware you won't approve all the time? How do they handle that?

Maybe you can relate to them as neither your babies nor as little children but as members of a family unit, each with different histories, skills, interests and responsibilities. They will forever be your children and you will always be their mother. Accepting that might free you all up to play with these roles as part of taking on the developmental challenge of continuing to build together a trusting relationship, a continuous family dance of difference.

Developmentally yours,
Lois

I Don't Want to Hurt My Dad, so I Stay Quiet

Dear Dr. Holzman,

I'm having a pretty hard time back at college this semester. I'm living at home with my Dad. We recently moved from New York to Costa Rica, where my Dad grew up. I've been here for vacations, but that's about it. I'm now in my second semester at college where everyone speaks Spanish.

My Spanish is OK, but not great. Academically it's hard, and so is trying to make friends. I don't feel like people can really get to know me. I think I must sound pretty stupid with my pathetic vocabulary. It's like being this outsider. Everyone keeps their distance. No one knows this, but I can actually be pretty funny in English, not just "stupid." That's a big part of my personality, but it's gone when I can't speak my own language.

At home, my dad (who's bilingual) speaks English. It's a relief, 'cause I can be more myself, and we can joke around. He'll ask me how it's going at school, but I can't tell him how miserable I am, 'cause I think he'll blame himself for us moving here and him putting me in this situation. So I choose "no comment." He wants me to have the benefit of both cultures and be bilingual like he is. But I'm not. I don't want to hurt him, and it's stressful.

Lost in Translation

Dear Lost,

I'm glad you reached out to me with a challenging situation that's painful for you. Moving to another culture and country at your age is hard enough. And you feel even more out of your element because you don't speak the language. I have some ways you might look at your situation from a somewhat different angle, ways that might give you a developmental path forward.

First off, I think you are not so much "lost in translation" as you are lost in your own head. You're feeling miserable because you're all alone with your identity and your assumptions about others and how they see you. You're standing in your own way. I invite you to take some steps toward others.

For example, you could ask your classmates for some help. You could tell them how you feel. You could tell them you feel stupid since your Spanish is so bad. You could tell them you're a pretty funny guy—in English—and ask them if they can help you be funny in Spanish too. I imagine this sounds scary! But I have a trick. It worked for me and maybe you can figure out how something like this might work for you.

Here's my story. Years ago, I was on my way to do some workshops with Russian teachers, something I had done a few times before. Part of me was dreading the trip because of how bad my Russian was, in spite of my efforts to learn to speak the language. I was determined to do something different so that I wouldn't go into my shell the minute the workshop ended each day and small talk began.

During the first break the first day, I asked five of the students (all of whom were Russian teachers of English) to "play" with me for an hour. The game we played was "Lois teaches you Russian." That's right. I was performing as a teacher of Russian! Armed with one question, "How do you say 'how do you say …' in Russian"—which I asked over and over and over—we created an introductory lesson that resulted in us writing a silly little poem.

What had I done? Well, I did learn a bit of Russian and the teachers said this game gave them ideas for their own teaching. But most important, performing as teacher changed my identity as non-speaker and brought me out of my feelings of inadequacy. The teachers and I felt much closer to each other having created something together.

And so, I think, can you become closer to your classmates if you find ways to talk to them and create something with them, in English and Spanish.

I also think that what you see as your problem might be an opportunity to build your relationship with your Dad instead of keeping him distant. Instead of shielding him with "no comment," be curious about him. Do you know how he became bilingual? As a child did he speak two languages or learn English later? How did he learn it? When he came to live in the US did he feel like people thought he was stupid? How did he handle it?

In a nutshell, my "advice" is to get lost with others!

Developmentally yours,
Lois

How Do We Help Families Navigate Computer Time?

Dear Developmentalist,

We do a lot of social therapy with families and kids. A big issue coming up in our groups are the growing conflicts and tensions around kids being online (on social media, making videos, playing games, hanging out in chat rooms, etc.) and parents becoming concerned, fearful, protective and laying down the law to limit their kids' access and/or monitor their activity. There are real fears: predators, bullies, scams, phishing, etc. It is the Wild West.

Parents also are concerned that their kids are "running away from their families"—staying glued to their phones and leaving parents feeling ignored at the dinner table.

On the other hand, there is a lot of what kids love about playing online that seems very positive to us: meeting other kids "across borders," making connections beyond their families and neighborhoods, and learning about the world. TikTokers are truly creative with their funny, playful videos and photos. Social media offers plenty of opportunity to be creative. And for kids in the LBGTQ community, it can be a lifeline to exploring sexuality in a healthy way.

We'd like to encourage families to approach the virtual world and new media as developmentalists—and so we're coming to you to ask you for your thoughts. We know that "laying down the law"—being punitive, fearful or performing as Luddites by trying to turn back the clock—is a recipe for fights and resentment. So how do we encourage all to engage and approach and use this technology to enhance their sociality—form new relationships—be more of and in the world— rather than zoom out into a private metaverse that leaves everyone alone, disconnected, alienated, depressed and worse?

Looking forward to your feedback,
Miguel Cortes, Ciudad Juarez
Barbara Silverman, NY

Dear Miguel and Barbara,

I'm so glad you took the time to write to me! The issue you describe is pervasive and will resonate strongly with parents and therapists and counselors who work with families, children and teens.

My responses to what you have shared are taking me in so many directions, I may not get to all of them in one response!

I wonder how *online time* became an "issue" (and a "big" one, at that) and a source of "growing conflicts and tensions." I don't mean only for the families you work with, but as a cultural phenomenon across much of the globe. So that's one area that I think is important to explore.

Perhaps, Barbara and Miguel, you might begin with your own histories and if and how new technologies became a source of conflict in your families when you were growing up. I'm thinking of the big deal television was when it became affordable for households. Then came cable with hundreds of channels, many of which were labeled and/or thought of as unsuitable for children and teens. The invention of the Walkman and the iPod made it possible for people to listen to music and other audio privately. Did your parents try to control the amount and type of material you watched and listened to? Can you recall how you felt and how the family dealt with the flood of content available to you?

Parents have always had a dilemma, it seems to me. They want to protect their children and keep them safe AND they want to give them opportunities to learn to take responsibility and think things through to their possible consequences. The issue today, as you describe it, is that navigating their way through this dilemma has become harder and harder. And it's just about impossible if you make it an either-or choice and try to deal with it by yourself.

You say you want to encourage families to approach the virtual world and new media as developmentalists—great! And yet, the gist of your letter is geared toward the parents and from the adult point of view. I suspect you have a vision of what a developmentalist approach might look like for the adults. For the young people, I am not so sure. Maybe you can put that on your therapeutic agenda. Ask for their support.

But it sounds like the social media activity is already treated special and off limits to parents. How did that get produced? This could be a place to start. Perhaps the developmental dilemma for parents and for you stems from treating the young people's phones, iPads, video games, and whatever else, as *theirs*, rather than as something *the family* has and uses (that, like most things, can be wonderful and also at times not so great). When they are little, kids have one relationship to stuffed animals and toys, and adults have a different relationship to them. But these things belong to the family and household, nevertheless.

Another area for you to explore is *family talk*. Do the parents talk with each other about their day and how they are creating their lives? If they're people who generally ask, "How was school today? How was practice? How was work? What did you do at your friend's house?" do they also ask, "Who did you meet online today, anyone new? How'd you do in Minecraft (or whatever game they like)? Did you discover anything today?"

Do the parents ask to learn their kids' games or to see what they liked on social media? And do they themselves share what they (the parents) are doing online and what they're discovering and who they're talking with on social media? Can they organize time to play together (parents and kids) finding something new online every day?

I hope that you will play with my wonderings and questions. I am sure that you can be of great help in furthering family talk. Creating new kinds of conversations is powerfully developmental for all.

And take a look at this site and decide if it's useful to you—Children and Screens (https://www.childrenandscreens.com/about/).

Developmentally yours,
Lois

CHAPTER 6
ON THE JOB

A Hostile Work Environment Is Killing Me!

Dear Lois,

I am living in China and work for more than 12 hours a day. When I was younger, this level of intensity was not a big deal, but now that I am older, it is really hard for me to handle. Working in a government agency has also been a big challenge. I find it difficult to play at this job—to be my old playful self—and feel like maybe I've lost my playfulness altogether.

The workplace is a bad political environment, and often makes me hostile. When we work with government employees, they may say "Yes" to my face, but in reality, many of them resist direction. Civil servants are all locals with local connections (even the driver has connections), and the government employees are intertwined with local politics too. I am the only outsider. It's like a spider web: They watch and wait for me to make a mistake.

How can I be playful in such a hostile environment? How can I welcome failure/mistakes in a situation where if I fumble, I will pay a high price? I am still working hard to try to find potential friends. I am still performing as being open to everyone I work with.

I hope I will have more hope/faith soon. Please share your thoughts.

P.L., China

> Dear P.L.,
>
> Thank you for writing me at a time when you're facing so many challenges. If I am reading you right, where you are living in China is new for you, and you have yet to develop friendships or a community that

DOI: 10.4324/9781003528364-8

can nourish you. This new location and situation itself must be so very hard! I assume that working in a government agency is also new for you—another big challenge! Not to mention that you experience it as a hostile environment. I have to wonder how you wound up in this situation and how come you don't leave. Do you have to stay? Or can you embrace that you made a mistake and reorganize your life?

Whether or not you can leave, I do think there's some growing you can do. I offer no promises that you'll "find" your playfulness again, but that might turn out to be OK. Maybe you can recreate it instead. Maybe your playfulness needs to look a different way in this new environment. Maybe the way you're used to playing doesn't work here. Maybe you need to "play around" with your performance of playfulness and create some new relationships to it and to the environment you're now in.

Since we usually think of relationships in terms of people in our lives—"I'm in a new relationship now"; "I have a good relationship with my father"—the notion that you have a relationship to your playfulness might seem odd or farfetched. But stay with me for a while.

So while we're in relationships with other people, we humans are always relational—with everything. We're in relationships with parts of ourselves, like our imagination, our hands and feet, our sadness, our fear. (Lots of people don't have a good relationship with their bodies, for example.) And then there's our environments—we have relationships with them too, like our home, our nation, our neighborhood, our job.

As soon as we step into a new environment, we're in a relationship with it. And it sounds like the one you're in with this governmental agency is pretty bad. Can you make it better? And what about your relationship to your playfulness? In this new environment, you feel you can't be "your old playful self." And you're probably right. But you can create a new relationship to your playfulness. You can learn to draw on it in different ways than in the past.

Get to know better the culture of the agency and who your workmates are. How do they play? What might they be open to from you? Your playfulness is as capable of becoming and growing and changing as "you" are. It needs to play!

Developmentally yours,
Lois

My Medical Patients Want Me to Be a Miracle Worker

Hi Lois,

I am a medical doctor, and I have many elderly patients with dementia. I have found the East Side Institute's *Joy of Dementia* programs to be very helpful for building ensembles and working with patients and their families. However, some patients for various reasons are not able to participate in such activities, and even if they are, like most things in life, it can still be very challenging. I would like to ask for your help with regard to my role as a doctor. I am supposed to be able to help the patient, when in fact the patient is deteriorating and medications are not going to cure the problems. I do not have answers for the patient and their family, but often they are expecting me to take care of the situation, but I cannot.

Thank you,
Doctor, NYC

Dear Doctor,

Thanks for writing. I've always thought that the challenges of doctoring are enormous due to the bureaucratic and institutional constraints placed upon the profession and, equally, due to the conflicted ways we are socialized to relate as doctors and patients. You are expected to know everything about illnesses and bodies and to be a miracle worker capable of fixing anything. I have such gratitude and respect for you and other physicians and appreciate the especially difficult situation you are experiencing when caring for elderly patients with dementia.

From how you describe things, I wonder if maybe you have bought in too much to the help = cure equation. It's the scientists and researchers, isn't it, who are working on finding cures (if, indeed, there are any) for dementia? Not clinicians like you—your job is to give care. You say you have no answers for the patients and their families, but that "they are expecting me to take care of the situation, but I cannot." What situation? That there is no cure? That the patient will not get better? That's not your fault! That they and their family don't know how to go on under these circumstances? That they are angry and sad and feel helpless? That's not your fault either, but maybe you *can* help them with this.

I'm urging that you not equate *having answers* with *taking care of the situation*. As a caring and experienced physician, you know all too well that their situation is more than their illness. It includes how they relate to and understand their illness and how they feel it as a family. Are there things they can build on in their history as a family? Who among them has which strengths and which weaknesses? What can you build on in your history with these patients? What are your strengths and weaknesses? Finding ways to talk with them about these things will help everyone break the non-developmental equation.

Developmentally yours,
Lois

I'm a Workaholic! What Do I Do when It's Time to Relax?

Dear Lois,

I'm coming out of an intense period at work. It's that time of year when there's a huge crunch! Then it lets up. For the past 3 months, my focus has been on crossing the finish line. All went well with the project, but it always impacts on my emotionality. Somehow life becomes smaller during such times. I am not organizing what I need as much as I would do in other times.

   The reason I'm writing is that when I come out of a period of intense work, I'm not quite sure how to go back to living at a regular pace and what to do with my extra time. Can you help?

Thanks,
Nose to Grindstone

Dear Nose to Grindstone,

First, congratulations on crossing the finish line!

   Second, thank you for writing and asking for help. I imagine many readers will recognize your situation of feeling a bit at sea after an intense period of work. I hope that this response helps them too.

   I felt a bit sad reading your letter because you sound alone with this. My feeling sad comes more from what you didn't say than from what you did. I imagine that you feel satisfaction and pride at coming through the crunch, but since you didn't mention it, I wonder what you "do with" satisfaction. Do you share it with others (or even with yourself)? Do you let it linger awhile and even savor it? Are you the only one that's been in this crunch or is there a team? Does the team share its satisfaction at crossing the finish line? Maybe it's worth talking with friends and co-workers and seeing what you discover together.

   You say that these crunch times always impact on your emotionality. No doubt they do. Could it be that *how* they impact has a lot to do with how you understand and relate to them? You say it's "that time of the year." To you, these periods are exceptions to what you experience as living at a regular pace. But if they happen year upon year, aren't they *part of your regular pace* rather than exceptions to it?

Your life consists of moving at different paces depending on work responsibilities of course, but also the seasons and time of year (and don't underestimate the holiday season and its impact on your emotionality!), your history, and the overall social-cultural context in which you are living. It's making the crunch times special and everything else "regular" that has you in this bifurcated world of yours, at a loss of how to use your "extra time." How limiting a life of crunches and lulls must be!

But it doesn't have to be yours. Because your life is a continuous process that includes crunch times and lulls and rain and blue skies and so much more. Really living it that way can be a developmental challenge of the best kind.

Developmentally yours,
Lois

I Can't Reach My Students: Maybe the "Villain" Role Will Work?

Dear Lois,

I am in my "villain era" with my students. I thought it was just what I needed to feel empowered as a professor! I have been committed to developing as an educator who believes in collaborative learning and the power of creating environments for all kinds of knowing. However, I've come to realize that some students have such an adverse reaction to a different teaching pedagogy that it has created a crisis.

I have strong reasons to say that being a "proper" woman in academia comes with lots of expectations: You must be caring, but not *too* caring. You have to accommodate—but if you don't—you are regarded as "difficult." And the list goes on. So, in response to being evaluated in a less-than-kind manner by students who adopted a consumer style approach as their way of relating to my teaching, I decided to become a villain. I cut my hair short (you know what I mean, right?). No more long-hair princess fairy tales. I am refuting the patriarchy.

Now as I get ready to go teach, I say to myself: This is me! I can access different ways of performing my work; I can make decisions; and I can still embody the principles of a collaborative pedagogy.

But that didn't solve the crisis. It feels that with one cohort of students I work with, there is nothing I can do to engage them. It is uncomfortable to be in their presence, as I can only describe their interactions with me as bullying. I've tried several approaches to overcome this pattern. I present ideas, have them engage in exercises, ask them questions, and all I get back is crickets, crickets (nothing!) and looks of discontent.

I know racism and sexism can be strongly present in interactions with students toward faculty, but I am hoping I am not right. What could I possibly do to enhance my superpowers in my "villain era" and not be affected by anybody's kryptonite? How?

In uncertainty,
D.

Dear D.,

I wonder if you will be reading this in your "villain era." I hope otherwise!

I appreciate you sharing your frustration. Our educational system—from the earliest years through higher education—breeds frustration, discontent and anger. And while most educators may well feel these emotions are righteous, my bet is that most feel, like you, that they don't do you, your students or anybody any good.

So, what can you do? A few things. But overriding anything you wind up doing is—don't do it alone! Talk to your students!

Did you tell your students in the frustrating cohort about your new performance (the "villain") or ask them what they thought of it? Have your spoken with them about how you're feeling powerless and asked them if they feel the same way? And have you told them that you can't solve this, but that only together can they and you come up with a different way to be together. (It helps to remind them that you are stuck with each other for this many hours each week and do they really want to spend that time being miserable, or mad, or bored, or ...?)

Listen to what they say and invite them to ask the "how" question: How can we go on together, given who and where we are?

Break a leg!

Developmentally yours,
Lois

Can I Be More of a Coach and Less of a Critic?

Dear Developmentalist,

I am a data scientist at a large financial institution that works with multiple technology vendors. I've faced challenges working with the people these companies provide.

One of the things that makes me tense-up the most in meetings is discovering: (1) that a situation is in a state more primitive than I had anticipated (lacking hygiene with respect to professional norms that directly impact the ability to achieve results of sufficient quality, and resulting in tangible and reputational loss for the business); and (2) that the supervisor in question has left it to me to coach and develop the team of young professionals, but without being their manager in any official capacity. My ability to set intent, provide critical reviews—to drive results—is attenuated in an environment where more is expected faster with less.

I sense the attitude among young professionals today is not inquisitive enough. They've adopted a more reclining posture, and their interim work products (if you could call them that) are whatever happens to come to their minds (e.g., critical self-assessment, peer review prior to submission to the client?), or (hope you like blank stares!) silence on the other side of the Zoom screen.

No one could credibly disagree with any number of theories: rote "learning" and standardized testing; "the climate crisis so what's the point-ism"; and easy capital, kombucha on tap; or "I can just get another job in 18 months, so whatever-ism"—to name a few.

That last part of the situation is cracking, thankfully, but in the meantime I've come to accept that my role is more coach than critic. I actually do get a small sense of accomplishment performing as a coach, but it's not sustainable given work timelines that have yet to acknowledge the mindset of early career professionals.

There's an element of managing up, too—I tell younger folks, "Your ideas are bad, and that's good!" And I need to learn how to tell senior leaders, "Your ideas are bad, and that's bad!"

What do you think?

Sincerely,
A.A. Manhattan

Dear A.A.,

Thanks for reaching out. I am particularly pleased that you've written to me at a time when you've begun some productive reflection on your environment, job and position. Seems like you're already in a process in which developing yourself and your relationships is potential. I wonder if you experience this. Maybe me pointing it out is helpful!

To me, it's significant that you've transformed how you understand your role at work from critic to coach and that you're getting some sense of accomplishment performing as a coach.

My advice is to fully own that. *Use it to build your relationships.* Instead of being critical (of both the senior leaders and the younger folks), perform more curiously to better understand their strengths and their limitations. It will make you a better coach, for sure!

Developmentally yours,
Lois

I'm a Leader without a Team, Now What?

Dear Developmentalist,

In my role at work, I am a leader without a team. I used to be one—but in the name of efficiency, my team's roles and responsibilities were outsourced across several vendors, and I've lost that connection with working with folks, day-in and day-out.

Now I am struggling a bit with how to show up as a leader. What I think of as leadership is having a team I see every day, people I know—who I could help to grow and who helped me to grow. It made what we did as a team "seeable" to our clients in support of their work. Now this new "team" of vendor support is still held to the same standards as my former staff, and it is my responsibility to ensure we meet those standards.

I think this requires a new form of leadership, one I am trying to build as I go, even as the concept of work is evolving for everyone. The *human element* is less visible. After a few years of everyone being remote, clients are returning in mixed remote and in-person environments which is new for them, and new for us. Our clients need to grow in this new scene, and we, as a new team, need to grow with them.

I really want to show up as a new kind of leader, one who is not leading a team but creating one, and I want to do this with our clients and with our vendors, not as a transactional relationship, but as a group who's building something new.

Andrew, Brooklyn, NY

Dear Andrew,

I'm glad you wrote me to share your challenging situation at work. As I understand you, you had a team of people at your company that you led and now you are needing to lead a group of outsourced vendors and to do that primarily virtually. I'm happy to hear that you recognize that *the team doesn't exist yet*—you have to create it. Actually, not *you* alone, but you and the vendors and clients.

My guess is that this issue of how to lead was the big unknown for organizations and their people during the COVID lockdown and remains so post-lockdown. I deliberately call it "unknown."

After all, how could they or anyone know how to lead in a changed world? In a virtual space? When all aspects of work became dependent on technology? But hardly anyone chose to admit not knowing what to do and to seize the opportunity to create it together. Now, that would have been leadership appropriate to the transformed situation!

Instead, some tried to simply take their leadership style online, others proclaimed this or that existing leadership style was what was needed, and still others invented new styles (complete with books, blog posts and TEDx talks).

Tell your people *you don't know how to lead them* (especially since they don't directly work for you), and that this is not a personal failure but rather a *collective opportunity*. Tell them you couldn't know, because you don't yet know them nor they each other, and that it's a new situation. Tell them, "Together we will discover how to create our team." Talk to them. Find out what they want and what they need. Discover together what their strengths are and if they want to do this with you and each other.

Just as virtual and hybrid work environments are new physical spaces, they are also *new relational spaces*. I think we fail to appreciate their potential when we see them comparatively, as less than what was, as deficient in "the human element" as you put it. The human element is vastly more complex and creative than the parts of it we experience when we are in the same room. Let's exercise our relationality, our smarts, our productivity in new ways. With your strong desire for group building and creating together, I think one developmental step you could take is to let your people in on who you are and are becoming. My guess is they'll appreciate that kind of leadership.

Developmentally yours,
Lois

CHAPTER 7
FRIENDSHIP

My Best Friend Won't Talk to Me When She's "Processing"

Dear Developmentalist,

My close friend and I talk regularly and talk about most everything. Recently she has started telling me that she wants to "process" events of her day/week/life before we talk about them.

It seems like this word "process" is being used everywhere and refers to someone's internal metabolizing of events affecting them, happening to them so that they can settle on a story of what happened.

Now, when my friend and I speak, she describes her processing to me—what she thinks really happened, what caused what to happen. Honestly, I find it distancing. Where is our old back and forth where we could say anything to each other, change our minds on what was happening, and trust that the other was accepting and present of the conversation we ended it?

Is there some loving way to challenge what I take to be the point of processing—which is to develop a certainty within oneself of "what happened" before speaking with anyone about it? Or am I processing "processing" incorrectly??

Thank you!
Meghan, New Mexico

Dear Meghan in New Mexico,

I haven't come across what you're describing in terms of "processing," although the desire to settle on a story of what happened is certainly familiar. The need to make sense of events in our lives can

DOI: 10.4324/9781003528364-9

be overwhelming, and people can go to great lengths to convince themselves and others that they know what happened. I suspect that some of what's behind this need is the belief that we can't go forward without it.

You say that the change in the conversations you have with your close friend are due to her wanting to process events before she talks with you about them. Now, when you two speak, she describes her processing to you. You imply that you used to do this together, and you miss the freedom and trust of the back and forth of how your conversations used to be. You feel distant.

Meghan, I think distance is the key here, and it's good you identified it. But you might well be on the wrong track in assuming that it's your friend's "processing" that's distancing. (Is that a bit of "your processing," I wonder?)

I suspect that it's you not telling her that you miss how you two used to talk that's distancing. You ask, "Is there some loving way to challenge what I take to be the point of processing." I wonder why you would want to put this challenge to your friend (even if you could do so lovingly). I would think that it would increase rather than decrease the distance between you. Telling her what you love about your friendship with her, I suspect, would be more loving!

Developmentally yours,
Lois

Can I Be There for My Friend When I'm Also in a Lot of Pain?

Dear Lois,

As do a lot of us, I'm experiencing the world as becoming more crazy every day. In many ways it's an emotional roller coaster. I am a developmentalist, too: I work in my life to be fully present and responsive to others. My question to you is how can you make room for someone else's pain when it's so hard to deal with your own? And how can I share my fear and sadness in a way that makes space for others to hear it? With many of my friends, we have grown closer since the pandemic began, sharing ups and downs and moments of pain and stress over these last 2 years.

But sometimes it feels that others have a "full tank" when I want to talk to them about what I am going through. I don't want to overwhelm friends with my concerns when I can see they are also struggling. How do we go through all of what we're confronting together? How do you keep building spaces to grow with people close in your life when maybe both/all are overwhelmed?

R.S./Brooklyn, NY

Dear R.S.,

I appreciate you sharing your dilemma, a situation that must resonate with our readers. Whether or not the world is more crazy today (this year, this decade, this century) than it was yesterday (last year, last decade, last century), you're not alone in experiencing that it is. I'm not into comparison, though, and I don't think you are either. (Comparing too often becomes a constraint on creativity.)

You say that, as a developmentalist, you work to be fully present and responsive to others, and you describe when and how that feels hard for you. In my experience, it's always helpful and potentially developmental to play around with what we mean, so I invite you to explore with me "fully present." Usually it means "in the here and now"—that is, in the present. And, by implication, not in any other time or place, that is, not in history. For me, being present means being historically present, which is a different kind of here and now than the present moment.

What this could look like for you is that you and your friends might transform your conversations in such a way that you're all better able to handle feeling overwhelmed and continue to give to and support each other. For example, you might explore together how you understand being overwhelmed, how you understand pain, how you understand the relationship between them, and— how come you talk about them so much! I don't mean to sound harsh, but it's worth exploring when and how pain became so dominant in our conversations, both public conversations and ones with people we have close relationships with. In creating these new conversations, you and your friends and loved ones might come to realize that our experiences of being overwhelmed and of pain are continuously shaped and reshaped culturally, and that in our culture we're socialized to see, feel and respond to pain as individual and private—"This is my pain and that's yours."

Hmmm ... Aren't they both ours?

In addition to the assumption that pain is private, I wonder if your wonderings are related to the idea that we each have a "pain threshold" and "pain container"—as when you ask, "How can you make room for someone else's pain when it's so hard to deal with your own? And how can I share my fear and sadness in a way that makes space for others to hear it?" It might be a relief to imagine that there's no container, space or room in which we keep or put pain. Pain is, developmentally speaking, much better understood as an activity rather than a private mental state.

You ask a great question: "How do we go through all of what we're confronting together?" And the answer is right there in your question! Do it together. Socially, relationally, together—discover how you can do this together. That's the developmental way.

Developmentally yours,
Lois

I Have Endless Judgments about an Annoying Friend

Dear Developmentalist,

I am in a place in my life (at age 55 and the daughter of Chinese immigrants, coming back to the workforce after 16 years as a stay-/work-from-home mother) where I am working my ass off to grow, to have more—to see my partner as a *whole person*, and to see myself as a whole person.

Last weekend, I went to a spa with my girlfriends, one of whom put together the outing and invited someone my other girlfriends didn't like. When they heard she was coming, two of them cancelled. While I sympathized, I was disappointed that they pulled out, after all my hard work to create the group.

The next day, my friend told me that I had been "kind of negative," "tough" and "judgmental" with the (difficult) woman. She was right. I see this person as superficial, unselfconscious and anti-developmental. Her cluelessness is to the point where she questioned outright how come it was important to be self-aware. For me, self-awareness is key to everything.

I had asked her if she was happy, and she said she was "*sooo* happy," and described all the ways she was "living the best life," all while using (I thought) superficial metrics.

"I'm *sooo* happy with my career! … I'm having the best time. I love myself and no longer want a (romantic) relationship." When I asked, "Don't you want love?" she said, "Men are *meh*; I use them to service my sexual needs, but after sex I tell them to leave."

She's telling herself who she is in the world and is pretty smug about how great her life is. But what about how her friends see her? Doesn't the group see you in ways that you can't? Yet, she doesn't seem interested in listening to us telling her who she is.

Although I was trying to be present at the spa and focus on building the group, I was also indulging my judgments of this annoying woman—keeping my distance—and looking for reasons *not* to like her. But when my friend told me she could see me being judgmental, I felt like a hypocrite. I had stopped looking for opportunities to grow. How can I create development out of this situation?

C.S., Manhattan

Dear C.S.,

Thanks so much for asking me directly for help with what you shared about being judgmental. It sounds like you've done a lot of work on this in your struggles to see and relate to "the whole person." I think that's wonderful! From what you tell us about your conversation with your friend the day after the spa visit, you also take to heart how others see you. That, too, is wonderful!

What's not so wonderful, however, is indulging your judgments, although it's wonderful you're aware you did that and feel bad about it.

I wonder what happened to "seeing the whole person" when it came to this "difficult" woman. It might be worth exploring why you chose not to do so with her. Was there something about the environment, the spa, your friends, this woman, how the visit was organized, why you wanted to go and what you were looking forward to?

What's developmental when it comes to judgments is not to try to get rid of them. We all have them—thousands of them hundreds of times a day. Judging is part of being human. The issue is not *that* we have them but what we do with them. I suspect that, like most people, you think that when we have judgments about people, those judgments have to color how we interact with them, and that we have to get rid of the judgments in order to be caring, responsive, curious, etc. with that person.

But we don't. At least that's my experience. When I find myself vulnerable to *acting out* judgmentally toward someone, I make a choice to *perform* instead. To do a different performance with that person, something other than all the negativity I feel. And sometime later, I perform being judgmental; I play with my judgments. What does that look like? Well, sometimes I make up a song or poem about how annoying that person is and sing or say it to myself. Sometimes I go on a rant, passionately sharing with someone all the things that bother me—not unlike how you've written to me about this woman!

Ranting is a healthy thing to do—IF you do it intentionally, performatorally (and away from the person you're ranting about)!

Developmentally yours,
Lois

CHAPTER 8
GRIEF AND LOSS

I'm Overwhelmed with Grief over My Son's Illness

Dear Lois,

Four years ago, my child was diagnosed with a condition that has resulted in rapid progressive disability. We have been fortunate that the auto-immune part of this condition has not yet materialized, but we have to constantly be on the watch for cancers and lung related illnesses. In one year, he went from being a child who could run, was learning to write, etc., to someone who is completely immobile, unable to write or draw, needing to be fed by others, etc.

As parents, we ensure our family lives a full creative life, and find contexts for all our children to thrive. This child is no exception and is happy and thriving. Yet, there is the ongoing grief that goes with supporting a child with this kind of condition, and the various battles with health institutions, educational institutions etc. My dilemma is this—that this is not our or his "tragedy" (alone) and that it should be shared with our family and close friends. But our support base is very minimal. I have friends who never ask or touch base. We have close family members who act as if there are no issues or stresses with his condition—even when told that he needs to have medical tests, or be taken to the hospital, or must have an operation. My work colleagues have never engaged with me at all about him or me or us, even after I have told them about the situation.

I also know that we need to live each day and create each day. However, I get really anxious about the future—and how to navigate it. How do we navigate the ongoing sense of loss that this kind of condition

DOI: 10.4324/9781003528364-10

confronts us with daily, whilst living a full life, and whilst psychologically preparing for the next "thing" on the horizon? How do I find ways to share this with friends and family, and the energy to ask for help when often I do not know what I need, but know that everyday grief is hard?

A., Cape Town, South Africa

Dear A.,

I am touched that you wrote me about your son's condition and its impact on him, you, and the rest of the family. The care he needs, the constant vigilance and worry of further deterioration, the feeling of loss, and the sadness of even greater loss to come … all of this colors and shapes your lives-as-lived now. My heart reaches out to you.

You also tell us that this transformation hasn't destroyed or replaced how you all had been doing family before his illness—creating contexts and activities for your children to thrive and for all of you to live fully and creatively. That seems so important to me. Here's why. It sounds to me like your son's illness isn't *all-consuming* in taking over and not allowing for doing and feeling and thinking about anything else. It sounds more like you all are doing your best at being and becoming—that it's not all-consuming, but is *all-encompassing*. I don't know if this distinction is helpful or comforting to you, but your letter and your situation move me to say it.

You describe your "dilemma" as understanding that "this is not our or his 'tragedy' (alone) and that it should be shared with our family and close friends," and yet having a minimal support base. That must make such a difficult and demanding situation so much harder. It is a big move to ask (me) for help with this.

You write about "friends who never ask or touch base. Close family members who act as if there are no issues or stresses with his condition, and work colleagues who have never engaged at all about him or me or us, even after I have told them about the situation." You want to bring them closer. You want to share with them what it's like, and you want to ask for help even when "I do not know what I need but know that everyday grief is hard?"

I wonder what your conversations with these friends and family members and co-workers are like. Do you tell them how you feel when they are distant? Do you invite them to share with you how they feel when you tell them both bad news and good news? Do you ask them what they need to be closer to you? And do you ask them for help even when you don't know what you need—inviting them to help you *discover* what you need?

I think it will take courage to create these kinds of conversations. You will be vulnerable. Some people might be rejecting. Some others will thank you. And perhaps the energy you are seeking will come from making your support group a little (or a lot) bigger.

Developmentally yours,
Lois

Cycling Was My Happy Place, and Now That's Gone

Dear Lois,

I'm middle-aged and actively fit. But these days, the heat and humidity knock me out; I get tired more easily; I have a lot less "get-up-and-go."

I used to LOVE to ride my bike—it's how I spent most of my free time. I loved to feel the breeze on my skin. I loved to cruise down a tree lined path. It was my happy place and my happy activity. And it was kind of obsessive too—pushing, pushing, pushing to complete the miles. Sometimes very painful. Slogging to the finish line. Sometimes I'd ride an extra loop around the parking lot just to get the odometer to hit my goal.

And it was kind of isolating and lonely, too—some days I'd spend 6 or 7 or 8 hours alone on a bike tooling through the countryside or in the suburbs.

My group of friends who used to bike together have all moved on—to other cities, other activities.

But now, contemplating the joy I use to find on the bike (almost crying in remorse!) I can't make myself go out and do it. It's too hot. It's too humid. It's too scary. The trucks are too big. The scooters too fast. (A woman on a scooter drove head on into me a few months ago. We both went down.) I'm even more scared now—of aggressive head-on collisions. The social environment has changed since the pandemic— more motors, faster, more super aggressive.

When I think of getting on a train or renting a car to get out of the city to bike, I give up, contemplating how tired I'll be just carrying my bike to the train platform.

Wow. This is a big problem. My great source of joy is no longer. I'm exercising other ways—Pilates, dancing, aqua aerobics. But nowhere is the joy I found in biking. This is very sad to me.

I'm in a completely confused muddle. Hope you can help.

Cycler in the City

Dear Cycler in the City,

I'm glad you wrote to me for some help with your confused muddle.

I wish everyone would write me when they're in the maze of confusion. It really does help. Even if you never send the letter!

Write down what's confusing you and read it out loud a few times. You'll experience something changing in relation to your confusion. Maybe the fog will begin to lift a bit.

Now to your muddle.

You have a complex set of emotions in relation to biking, both in the past and now. It used to be a great joy. You loved it. It was lonely. It was isolating. You were obsessive. Today, you no longer want to bike, it's too scary, people are too aggressive, and just thinking about it is exhausting. I suspect that's part of your confusion—loving and hating, wanting and not wanting, feeling so alive and feeling so alone.

We humans so often feel more than one thing at a time—about what we're doing, about ourselves, about others, about the world … And why wouldn't we? We are indeed complicated! The confusion, I think, is not in the messiness of emotions but in our belief in and need for them to be neat and tidy.

The psychological culture that shapes our beliefs and needs is, I suspect, producing your muddle in another way as well. You write that biking, your great source of joy "is no longer." I ask you, Cycler, how can that be? Are you saying that because you no longer bike that the joy you and it created for so many years has disappeared? That who you are and are becoming now doesn't include that joy? If it didn't, then how can it be that you miss it?

Just because you're not biking now, are you not a biker? Here, again, you're confused. After all, you did sign your letter, "Cycler in the City" even though, you tell us, you no longer cycle in the city! Maybe you're a biker—better yet, a joyful biker—who's not biking.

Developmentally yours,
Lois

I'm Anxious about Losing All That's Dear to Me

Dear Lois,

I've noticed that in many areas of life, I can "know" I'm in a good situation but have trouble fully appreciating it emotionally. How can I get better at appreciating the things without having to lose them first, in order to know what I have? A great example is my current job with a tech and design company. If I lost this job, I'd feel intensely how lucky I had been to have it. But without actually losing it, I can't connect emotionally to that. It's all theoretical.

Growing up, I would have done anything to be able to do art and design professionally. I didn't have any idea how to get into the game and never thought it would be a reality. But it happened. When I started at this company, I remember thinking that I'd happily sweep the floors all day to simply be there. I feel quite sure it is the best place I will ever work. It's pretty amazing. I like the work I do and the people I work with: they prioritize family and give lots of flexibility and time off. There are few artificial obstacles to growth, they encourage proactivity and independence, and they even encourage you to use some of your workday on personal art projects (which is practically unheard of in this industry). It's more than I think anyone could expect from a job!

But after many years, while I honestly feel happy there, I take lots of things for granted. I worry about the petty things—like who is in what position relative to my own. My position at the company is ideal. I have a lot of independence and leadership responsibilities. And I have the flexibility to make the role what I want it to be. There are a few positions senior to me, but they are way more stressful and wouldn't allow me to lean into my strengths as much as I can now. But the competitive part in me wants to "move up" even though I'm almost certain it would be a reduction in quality of life.

Lois, I notice this in other areas of my life too (not just the job), and I want to find a way to more deeply appreciate what I have without having to learn the lesson the hard way through loss.

All the best,
B.A., Michigan

Dear B.A.,

Thank you for writing me and sharing some of your worries. You say you want to appreciate more deeply what you have in your life, and that got me thinking about appreciation. Maybe if I share some of my musings with you it might help you make some discoveries about your own relationship to appreciation and to your life, including your emotional life.

I think lots of people will relate to what you're describing— feeling overjoyed by some things in your life and then, after some time passes, taking those very things for granted. I think the reason this is so common is that we become distant from our lives. We forget that we created the circumstance that elated us (and also the elation). In your case, you never thought it could happen that you could be a professional designer. "But it happened," you say. Well, B.A., I don't think so! It's just not that simple. Whatever the process was and however long it took, you played a big role in creating your professional life as an artist and designer.

I think you've forgotten that. Or maybe you were never aware of it during the process of getting your dream job. Not knowing/ experiencing/"having" one's own involvement means we're alienated from ourselves as creators of our lives. Without this particular "sense of self," we often stop continuously creating our life's circumstances.

I suspect that's what's happening with you, B.A., and that's how come you're taking the job for granted, feeling guilty about that, worrying about losing the great gig you have, being petty and berating yourself for that, and so on. When you begin to feel that things happen TO you, rather than you being part of making them happen, you stop appreciating what you have. And you stop appreciating yourself.

My advice? As a veteran artist and designer, it's time you appreciate the art and design that goes into creating your life. What a great project!

Developmentally yours,
Lois

"You Can't Go Home Again"

Dear Lois,

I am hoping you can help clear the mental mist. I am handicapped by the relationship to "my past."

Background: I'm listening to "A Gentleman in Moscow," a story about a Russian aristocrat who's living under house arrest at the grand Hotel Metropol. He shares observations about the sweeping changes in the life of post-revolutionary Russia, along with vivid memories from across his life. The gentleman does not appear to be handicapped by his emotions and so is able to wring rich, detailed memory from every inch of his life. He owns/recalls his entire life (even under confinement). That is in such contrast to the poverty of how I relate to a lot of my (painful) life history.

I've been visiting my "hometown" in the south where my father and his relatives are from. My family went on summer vacations here when I was a girl, and I went to college here. Even though it's decades later, my visit is shrouded with the emotionality of yesteryear—an emotional memory/uneasiness that colors the NOW. It's like hearing an old song and being "transported" to that time in your life—as if you're there again. It's pretty child-like—all about me—transported back in time in this anxious fog.

I would like to be able to play, have, narrate, build with, give my past—and not be stuck in an aversion to reliving it, emotionally speaking. If you can help with this, I would be very grateful.

"You Can't Go Home Again," NY

Dear Can't,

I was glad to receive your letter asking for some help with your relationship to your past. I'm eager to explore (and maybe help to clear) your mental mist—a condition so pervasive among humans that sometimes I think it might be a universal condition.

This might take a while, so bear with me.

You sign your letter "You Can't Go Home Again"—the title of a novel by the American writer Thomas Wolfe that's become a well-known saying in English. I wonder what that means to you. Who is the "you" that can't go home again? What is the "home" you cannot go to again? Whatever home is to you, it's not there anymore.

Because home, as you of course know, is not a physical-geographical space. And who are you? You are an adult who, upon visiting a city of your childhood, is "shrouded with the emotionality of yesteryear … hearing an old song and being 'transported' to that time in your life, as if you're there again."

That's not the you of yesteryear, and it's not the emotionality of yesteryear either. It's the you-of-now, who has a past. And that past includes not only "what happened" but, equally impactfully, your experiences and understandings, interpretations and re-interpretations, and tellings and retellings (even if only to yourself) of stories of what happened. And it includes the emotionality that comes along with all that.

You say that, unlike the "Gentleman from Moscow" who "has his entire life," you are "handicapped by your emotions" and feel there's a poverty in how you relate to a lot of your (painful) personal history. Hmmm. Again, I wonder. Because you seem to me to have a rather rich emotional life related to that history. Perhaps too rich. I couldn't say. But, for better or worse, it's what you have created! I invite you to try that on and see how you feel.

The widely accepted notion of being handicapped by our emotions usually comes along with the need to get rid of them. I don't think that's a good idea, for you or anyone. First of all, I'm pretty sure it can't be done. But what if we created many more emotions? They would then also be part of our lives and live "side by side" with the ones we believe are handicapping us. And then you could "play, have, narrate, build with, give"—not your past, but all of you, including the "old" and new emotionality.

That would be developmental! That would be the way it is in our earliest years, when what we do with others in the present transforms our past.

My advice is to practice being childlike as a developmentalist (in this case, helping yourself develop). Your development just might include you no longer trying either to relive your childhood or avoid reliving your childhood. Or at least doing it less. There are so many more creative ways to live your life! I would very much like for you to have that.

Developmentally yours,
Lois

CHAPTER 9
AGING, DISABILITY, AND DYING

It's Difficult Navigating the Health Care System

Hi Lois,

I have been dealing with COPD for several years. Recently as I turned 65, I was diagnosed with another illness: chronic kidney disease. As I age, I am no longer able to do many things I used to do, like running, working a full-time job, eating certain foods, moving in certain ways etc. In addition to having a hard time letting go of these things, it is hard to let go of being youthful and having good health.

As I explore new possibilities in how I live my life, it is difficult not only to handle the above but also to deal with the medical maze of doctors, specialists, drug regimens, etc. I often receive contradictory answers from doctors, and the more I talk to doctors about what to do, the more overwhelming it feels.

My question is: How do I let go while navigating health options in what feels like a wasteland of decision making?

Developmentally yours,
Howard

Dear Howard,

Thank you for sharing these aspects of your current life that are so difficult. Finding out you have a chronic illness (or two) is life changing. And so is having to immerse yourself in the dysfunctional

DOI: 10.4324/9781003528364-11

US health care system. It's hard enough to no longer be able to do things you've always done. But now you're spending a lot of your time in doctors' offices and on the phone with medical folks of all kinds, often (as in your case) with very little satisfaction. Not a great way to live your life!

If you're like most people, the combination can feel life shattering. It needn't be. There are ways to feel less shattered, less in a wasteland, and less sad about no longer being young. Let's try a few out.

First—recognize, accept and embrace that you are not alone! And act on that recognition, acceptance and embracing. Getting older and getting sick aren't unique to you, nor is how you respond to it. Everyone gets older; most people acquire one or another illness. These universal human experiences feel to each of us uniquely individuated. And while they are individual, they are also and at the same time shaped by history, culture and society. I wonder what could happen if you were able to have both its universality and its Me-ness at the same time. Can you try?

Another way to embrace that you're not alone is to do your chronic illness, do your getting older, and do your medical exploring and navigating with other people. I suspect that most people get less social when faced with these life changes. But you need to be more social now than ever before! Do this life change with others. Create a health team. (From among your friends and family, invite a few people you trust and value.) Bring someone with you to doctor visits. Review and evaluate the medical recommendations and decide together how to proceed. I guarantee, from experience, that this kind of socializing your illness is developmental. I experience it as creating emotional strength.

I also wonder how you think about yourself. Are you still "Howard"? I wonder how much of your identity has been tied to what you used to do. I wonder if that's how come you speak of having to "let go." If I were you, Howard, I wouldn't let go of anything. Instead, I would let in everything.

Developmentally yours,
Lois

Is It Time to Retire from a Company I Founded?

Dear Lois,

I am now 70 and getting ready to retire (sooner than later). I run my own company and will be turning it over to my partner. She has asked me to stay on for one more year, which I'm thinking about doing. That said, while I enjoy the work, I am getting tired and eager to do some new things. My concern is that if I stay another year, I'd like to do it differently (less stress, less hours, more time away), and I'm not sure how to do that. I'd like to give more of the work and responsibility to my team and support them to make decisions without having to run them by me. And, I'm a bit leery that I won't be able to keep my hands off and let them make the moves they feel need to be made. I don't want them to feel second-guessed by me but empowered—so not sure how to both support them and not be overly involved.

I can use some help on this.

Many thanks,
S.F., New Jersey

Dear S.F.,

Thanks for writing and asking me for help. You're a lucky man—having a choice about when to retire is not something everyone has. Plus, you have the luxury of whether to make a clean break or ease out of your job over a year's time. I hope you notice that I have a *different take* on the situation you're in from what you actually said—and that's the beginning of my help!

From what you say, you see your situation as one in which you "retire now" or "stay on another year." You can do this, OR you can do that. What you may be overlooking is that *this* and *that* aren't just WHAT you do—they're equally HOW. (There's never been a WHAT without a HOW!)

How many ways are there to retire? Who knows? No one does, until those ways are created. And how many ways are there to "stay on another year"? You don't know. I don't know. No one knows, until you and your team create it.

You want to do new things and do "old" things differently. How wonderful! Relating to yourself, your company and its people is clearly at the top of your list. Wonderful again!

As I see it, supporting your team to take on more work and responsibility doesn't depend on you staying on. Maybe the best way is to leave and be a coach or advisor. Or maybe you stay, and *you* get coaching on how to be more hands-off. Or maybe … There are endless possibilities when you embrace the creativity that lives in HOW.

Developmentally yours,
Lois

I Need to Reinvent Myself, but That May Not Be Practical

Dear Lois,

I'm trying to reinvent myself professionally in my late 50s, and it feels like a challenge. I have worked for years in a position that has been just fine but has never made me shine. I haven't felt the true passion for my work that I imagine is possible. I have several obligations including a child and a mortgage making me feel very conservative in the options I consider. I have dreams and ideas about creating something entrepreneurial in a creative market. There are so many vectors of help that I can ask about here, but to give focus, how do I approach this in a way that unites practicality with growth choices, and how do I (developmentally) live with my anxieties about any level of risk?

Signed,
Anxiously Wanting to Be an Entrepreneur

Dear Anxiously Wanting,

Thanks for writing me. I appreciate you wanting to take on this challenge developmentally. Over the years, I have coached dozens of people who were changing jobs and/or careers, and most of them had no idea that this often grueling activity could be growthful So, you're beginning with a leg up!

That said, I think some of how you're approaching this might get in your own way. So let's explore!

The very first thing you said gave me pause—that you're trying to reinvent yourself professionally. It's a popular notion these days. Curious, I did a quick Google search and the first thing to come up was, "5 steps to reinvent yourself." I clicked on it. I kept going— clicking on "4 steps ...," "10 steps ...," and, my favorite, "How to reinvent yourself: 11 ways to become a new person." As I read on, I was pleasantly surprised to find that many steps offered some basic good (if obvious) advice, like assess what's positive about your life, look at your skills, and network. NONE, however, had anything to do with becoming a new person.

That's because you can't. You *can* keep developing. You *can* continue to learn. You *can* try out new performances of you. But you can't become a new person. **You can't reinvent yourself.**

My question is, "Why would you want to?" Approaching a job change or career move developmentally is a reshaping—not an erasing—of who you are and have been. It's a process of playing around with the being/becoming-ness of you.

It's playing around with your obligations and your dreams, with your anxiety and your entrepreneurial spirit. Maybe you'll be inspired to find your way into the creative market outside of the job that pays your bills.

You ask how to unite practicality with growth choices? That's an easy one! Stop seeing them as separate opposites. Choosing to grow is exceedingly practical!

Good luck in your adventure!

Developmentally yours,
Lois

I'm Panicked That I May Be Getting Dementia

Dear Lois,

My mother and sister both died from dementia. My sister passed just a few months ago, and while the pain of that lingers, I'm also thinking about myself. Am I now going to get dementia?

A few years back, I was diagnosed with epilepsy, because of a couple of unusual incidents (sleepwalking, etc.) Since then, I take medication and seem to be OK, but I'm often questioning myself: If I forget this or that, is it common/normal or an indication of something more serious? I get angry easily, nervous about traveling, write myself a lot of notes, etc. etc.

I don't want to verbalize these concerns to friends, because then I think they'll be watching me, checking me for indications, etc.

I have a neurologist and don't even want to raise these concerns with her, because that'll "go on my record."

This questioning myself, second-guessing, etc., is driving me crazy. Can you help?

Margaret (Michigan)

Dear Margaret from Michigan,

Thank you for sharing your fears and asking me for some help. Since you tell us that you're afraid to tell your friends or your doctor, I think it was a huge step to write and send your letter! I wonder, was it scary to do? How are you feeling having done it?

I ask, because your responses might help you with both your fears and your second guessing yourself.

So many people are in your boat (or a boat like yours). Dementia is in our face—the growing worldwide epidemic of the diseases that comprise this catch-all phrase, the narrative of tragedy and heartache, the medical news (and non-news), the search for causes and cures and, of course, our personal experiences.

We are all questioning ourselves, not only about whether forgetting someone's name or losing your keys means you're getting dementia, but about all sorts of things. The issue, developmentally speaking, is what we do with that questioning.

It seems that what you do with it is believe that it is driving you crazy. I don't think it is. I think your obsession, your pain, your "craziness" are the biproducts of intense privacy.

Let's take a look at that privacy. Maybe the most obvious— and most detrimental—aspect of keeping what's bothering you to yourself is that you then have only you to talk to! The categories you make, what you put in them, and the meaning (with a capital M) you give to them get fossilized. But who isn't nervous about traveling these days? 99% of people get angry easily. Many people write themselves notes. You've lumped these behaviors together with forgetting things and they add up to "Dementia." You get the picture?

The more you talk to yourself and no one else, the more you get stuck in doing your ways of talking and thinking and feeling over and over and over. That's deprivation! (And it could become boring.)

It's likely to do you good to speak to your friends and doctor. But even if you decide not to, there is something you can do relative to them. Ask yourself, "Would they tell me if they sensed some changes in how I am? Do we have a strong enough relationship?" If you can let them tell you how you are, you might be able to spend less time in your head and more in the life you're creating with others.

Developmentally yours,
Lois

I'm Scared of Dying. Can You Help Me Be Less Morbid about Death?

Dear Lois,

I want to speak with you about death and dying. For many years I was scared out of my mind; thinking of not being around, the transition into dying; seeing my parents up-close and personal with their bodies and health breaking down and eventually not being able to speak; wondering if they were experiencing pain. I have also seen friends of mine organize their death—organize how they want to die—and still live their lives as their health fails. I would like to have more of a philosophical (dare I say, positive) approach to death and dying, and I'm hoping you can help.

Thank you.
E.B.M.

Dear E.B.M.,

Thanks, E.B.M. This is a tough one! Death and dying are both universal AND particular. They're both inevitable AND indeterminate. It's not easy to relate to processes and events like these. We know we're going to die, but when? How? Why? And even though we all die, how we're socialized to understand and deal with it is culturally specific.

Everyone experiences death and dying. And everyone also experiences one or more of the feelings you describe. Some people, like you, think about it a lot. Others hardly at all (the experts will tell you that's denial, but I'm not so sure). There are many different religious and different cultures' understandings and customs surrounding death. There's voluminous medical and scientific research being done. And, of course, there's no shortage of psychological explanations for death anxiety. All of us, depending on "where" we are and where we came from, are influenced, shaped and, in many cases, overdetermined by these kinds of institutional rituals and knowledge.

For the most part, religion, psychology, art and science tell and show us that death and dying are part of the life cycle. There's tons of advice out there about coping, accepting and even embracing what is platitudinously referred to as "a natural and normal part of life."

I say, "So what?" How is that supposed to help you or your dying parents feel better? What's normal these days makes most of us more anxious, not less anxious! How did it come to be that identifying something as natural or as normal is assumed to comfort us? Does it comfort you, E.B.M.?

I think not. Perhaps that's why you're seeking a more "positive" approach. As you do so, it's important to see death and dying for what they really are—not simply moments in the life cycle or states of being, but activities people DO, social-cultural processes we engage in with others. And wherever we are, no matter our culture and history, we carry out these activities of death and dying (and worrying and mourning and grieving) through specific institutions, including those of religion, health care, the law, economics and psychology. The ways they have organized us to act and feel have come to seem natural and normal, while they are anything but.

You're not the only one, by far, wanting to do death differently. To help you in your journey, I suggest you spend time at The Order of the Good Death. It's an online content-rich source of educational, practical and inspirational material on transforming death, both personally and for humanity.

I'll end with some commonsense advice from Huey P. Newton, co-founder of the Black Panther Party in the US, who faced constant threats of assassination from the police and FBI in the 1960s: "You can only die once, so do not die a thousand times worrying about it."

Developmentally yours,
Lois

CHAPTER 10
"IT'S JUST ME ..."

My Coworkers Say I Talk Too Much!

Dear Developmentalist,

I have recently taken a new job trying to find my way onto a work team that is small, friendly, caring, smart and restrained. Small talk comes in the form of sports talk. I'm not a sports fan, so I can be silent during chit-chat unless I'm directly asked about myself. Also of note, I come from an ethnic background and family who are highly verbal.

Lately, I've done some "over-talking" in meetings. I thought I was sharing something interesting, but later felt I have rambled and that it's a problem. (It's actually not just a feeling—I have received feedback from the team. I'm sure they have discussed this privately.) I think of other times I have over-talked and feel embarrassed and humiliated. Leaning more into the shame, I sometimes feel I have nothing worthwhile to add anyway, that I lack expertise. I think of the song "Idiot Wind" by Bob Dylan (who can be so nasty, as I can be).

Overall, people at this job are being very kind and patient, and I really do appreciate the candid feedback. I understand that there is limited time in meetings and that we want to use the time efficiently and to develop the other team members who are younger and were hired for their (educational) pedigrees. They have all studied business/finance. I have not.

I've considered bowing out of meetings to simplify this sore spot, but that feels like it may result in my isolation. And, it seems important to keep learning more from them about business and finance.

DOI: 10.4324/9781003528364-12

I'd like to be more circumspect and hold my tongue. If I can become more deferential and listen more, it will also help in other areas of my life, where it seems to me that people (myself included) compete for time to speak. I think it's a worthy challenge!

I want to learn to pick my moments and my words more consciously. But here's the rub: I wonder if in doing so, I may disappear—become mousy and passive. Even with a fear of vanishing, I work to reign in the urge to speak, often failing and finding myself rambling. I go to self-diagnosis and wonder if this is toxic narcissism to want to so urgently speak my mind? What is that craving for attention? Maybe competition is the issue here?

I want a new way to perform, not mousy but quiet; not fake, but conforming. And at times, I find myself puzzling over whether this is an environment of growth and development for me, and how I can show up.

Signed,
Rambling

Dear Rambling,

Oh dear, what a muddle you are in! I'm so glad you shared it because even though your situation is specific the muddle isn't.

We humans have this marvelous capacity to be and to do, all the while observing ourselves and reflecting on our beings and doings. What a gift and what a curse!

It allows us to see ourselves and others and make use of what we see to discover and create all kinds of new things. It allows us to grow and to transform the world. That's the gift, without which you wouldn't be writing to me, much less thinking and feeling all that you are sharing.

I'm afraid you're experiencing the curse! You're overthinking, over-analyzing, and overinterpreting. It sounds like all the energy you're putting into trying to figure out if you're talking too much and what it might mean if you try talking less is paralyzing you. It's keeping you from making use of the very gift of observing and reflecting in its most simple and immediate way—*try talking less and see what happens!* You can't know what will happen until it happens!

Let your team in on it. They seem quite supportive, having already given you constructive feedback. Tell them how much you appreciate it. Share with them that you'll be trying out some new ways to participate in meetings and invite them to tell you how you're doing, what's working, what's not. I think that you might discover that listening is not holding your tongue or being deferential or circumspect. Far from it. Listening is another gift we use to create relationships and belonging.

If you do this, you'll be creatively imitating your nine-month-old self. You didn't worry then that you might become mousy or vanish if you developed other ways than screaming and crying your eyes out to tell people you're unhappy, hungry or in pain, or want attention. By trying out new performances of yourself with the support of those around you, you blossomed, got "bigger" and contributed to your own becomingness and the creating of your family.

You can still do that, Rambling!

Developmentally yours,
Lois

I'm a Conflicted Romantic—I Still Want a Relationship

Dear Developmentalist,

Ever since I was a little girl, I have loved the idea of romantic love that I learned from TV and from relationships around me. I am in now in my 20s and have never had a relationship of my own, but I crave it and really want to experience that kind of love. I have had crushes, but I always received clear signals that the other person was not interested. Throughout the years, I've just let life "happen": school, work, family, other commitments. And I know that relationships take hard work.

At this point in life, I am not sure what to do. Part of me wants to just forget the idea of a romantic relationship and just keep going through life, and if it happens, it happens. Another part of me is holding onto the romance idea and thinking about how I could make it happen.

It doesn't help that I have always been on the heavier side. I know it's a reason for men not to see me as attractive (people have made unsolicited comments about my weight). Recently, I started a weight loss journey, purely for health reasons. That said, I do not want someone to be with me just because I am attractive; I want to be liked for who I am, the way I am.

Thank you,
A somewhat hopeless, yet hopeful, romantic

Dear Romantic,

Thanks for writing to share your worries (and other feelings) about romantic relationships. You are not alone in wanting one! Nor in worrying someone might like you for the wrong reasons. Nor in worrying that you're not the right weight to be considered attractive. Surely these are in the top five of worries women in their twenties (and thirties, forties, and so on) have! That's a sad and very painful characteristic of our current world. Judging from popular culture, though, I do think that this is changing for the better, but very slowly.

What I think I might be able to help you with is how you understand and, therefore, relate to your situation. Maybe my wonderings will offer other ways to see who you are and the situation you're in and suggest some new possibilities for what to do and how to be.

Let's begin with "letting life just happen." You mention aspects of your life—school, work, family, and other commitments—in this way. It's a common experience for us to feel that we've had no role in creating our lives, even though we've been active participants in going to school, getting a job, relating to our families, and so on. We may not be happy with what we've created, but that doesn't negate the fact that we did it. So, when it comes to a romantic relationship, you've set it up as either seeing if it happens or making it happen. That's the kind of dilemma that can keep you stuck.

What if, instead, you decide to live your life developmentally, which means entering spaces that are new to you and trying out performances that are new for you. The key thing, in my experience, is being open to building relationships with all kinds of people, with as little judgment of yourself and others as possible. When new things emerge, you have more possibilities to create something with them.

Moving on, you want to be liked for you who are. Let's play with that concept. Who are you? From my developmentalist point of view, you are not simply who you are now, but also who you're becoming. That's unknown, of course, until you become! But I'm certain that in the becoming process you don't lose who you are—you keep becoming **you**.

Finally, you describe yourself as a somewhat hopeless yet hopeful romantic. I invite you to try this on: Keep the romantic but drop the hopeless and hopeful. Instead, create hope. It's not only possible—it's essential for romance!

Developmentally yours,
Lois

I'm the Most Experienced Person in the Room, so How Do I Learn?

Dear Lois,

Recently I signed up for a drawing class at the Rhode Island School of Design. Though I currently make drawings when I need to, I do not have a drawing practice where I am drawing every day and developing my skills. Now that I have a minute, I thought, "Hey, take a drawing class! That will get you going!" I am sure that there is a lot of potential for this class to set me on a course to be drawing daily. The only trouble is, I know myself. I am the consummate "know it all." Knowing really gets in my way of discovering what is possible and learning new things.

My main goal for this class is not to be a "know it all." I know you know a lot about knowing and not knowing, and I thought you could give me some performance coaching on how to actually execute my plan of "not knowing" when every fiber of my being says: "Hey, I already know that."

Thanks, Lois
J.D., Rhode Island

Dear J.D.,

Congratulations on taking this step! There's nothing like doing something socially, with others—whether or not you already know how to do it—to get you going! Taking the drawing class can open up all kinds of possibilities for developing your discipline, your skill and your talent.

First off, doing what you already know how to do, but in a new context, *isn't* doing the same thing. It's doing a different thing. Drawing in a drawing class will be a new drawing practice for you, if you let it.

Think of it as relational, not solitary. You and the instructor (and other students if it is a group class) are doing drawing together. Try to see and experience that—the social-cultural activity, if you will—rather than seeing and experiencing yourself doing some specific things with pencil that you already know how to do.

If you let the newness of the activity and relationality of this situation drive your performance, the "know-it-all you" might be relegated to a minor role in the scenes you're creating (on paper and off).

And remember, J.D., have fun!

Developmentally yours,
Lois

I Can Be a Snob: I Keep Myself Distant with My Big-City Judgments

Dear Dr. Holzman,

I live in a small, quaint village on the outskirts of Philadelphia, not Center-City and not the suburbs. It's a little pocket of a town where many families have lived proudly for generations. Most are freely friendly and, well, neighborly. We say hello on dog walks, welcome new neighbors and say goodbye to those leaving. We talk with each other on our porches, make casseroles for one another during the trials and tribulations of life, and take in each other's mail.

However, if there were a "neighborliness grade," I would probably get a "C," at best. For example, I sometimes skip the "Hi theres" when walking the dogs; I don't join the block parties; and I don't make any effort to remember names. It's not that I don't also say "Hi" sometimes and make the periodic casserole, but I am certainly not fully in the mix. At a neighborhood gathering recently, several people asked me what it's like to be new in town. (Whoops, I have lived here for 20 years!)

You see, there is also something quite conformist and "frozen-in-time" about this town that makes me want to keep my distance. There are Halloween rituals, for example, dating back 100 years that everyone seems to know about but me. Young parents raising their kids also grew up in this town, as did their parents. There is something insular about the politics and culture. So I cast myself in the role of being different, not from here and a dedicated non-conformist.

You can see perhaps my dilemma for which I ask your advice Dr. Holzman. I keep myself separate from the community with my judgments, assumptions and labels. In my holding back in neighborliness, I think things like: I am radical & unconventional in how I live politically (passionately independent) and personally (in a multiple partner-with-no kids lifestyle), don't fit the mold of "these conventional people." I'm thinking, they don't want to know me, nor I them. For years I hid behind being busy and an introvert as a quick explanation for my stand-off-ishness. But more honestly, there is a part of me that likes to keep my distancing assumptions about the town and who lives here. After all, it might be unsafe to be closer, who knows? At the same time, I would like to be more open, curious, less guarded and, well, more neighborly. Help!

J.B.

Dear J.B.,

I loved reading about your developmental dilemma. We've all been there, more times than we can imagine! By "there" I mean in a role and an identity that doesn't work for us the way it used to. But at the same time, it isn't so constricting or painful that we're desperate to give it up. So, we stay in it and make up justifications for doing so. At some point, these justifications, too, become unsatisfying. I think you're at that place now, and so I appreciate you reaching out to me.

My first thought on reading your letter was that you sound alone in your dilemma. Which strikes me as odd, given that you live with other people with whom you share a "radical and unconventional" lifestyle. I wonder where they are in your dilemma. How do they participate in the community? Do they share your discomfort and trepidation and what sounds like arrogance? Do they, too, "hold back in neighborliness"? Is that how they experience you? Do they share your "distancing assumptions about the town"? If you all don't talk together about all this, you're missing an opportunity to continue to create your lives together and with your neighbors, in whatever ways you choose to do so.

You say that you "would like to be more open, curious, less guarded and, well, more neighborly." I don't want to read too much into your words, but you didn't say that you "should be ..." If this is really something you want, rather than something you feel obligated to do, then the choice is yours to change your character. After so many years of playing the same role on this community stage, it sounds like you're tired of it and want to try something new. Go for it (and be sure to ask your unconventional family to support you)!

You might begin by picking someone whose way of being open, curious, neighborly, etc. appeals to you and creatively imitate that person. See how that new performance feels, how it impacts your assumptions, what the response is (including your own), and what new possibilities it creates. Who knows? You might become a "new neighbor"!

Developmentally yours,
Lois

I'm Frustrated by My Students' Passivity

Dear Developmentalist,

I teach academic writing to a diverse group of college students in New York City. Two of my classes had an assignment to research, write and present on a topic of their choice, and about 25% of them chose: "the negative mental health implications of social media."

Their class presentations focused heavily on how social media can become addictive and contribute to depression, anxiety, loneliness and isolation. Most of what they reported echoed/rehashed the "conventional wisdom" reported in academic journals and the news media. Literally every student agreed with these points and voiced similar experiences and concerns. Some used psychiatric buzz words to describe the negative impact of social media activity. It was unanimous.

As their teacher, I am struck by (concerned about and frustrated by) the *passivity* and maybe even *victimization* of their responses, i.e., seeing Big Tech as the Actor/Creator; while the rest of us are merely users/consumers at their mercy. And I am worried that my responses could be off-base, trite and maybe irrelevant given the mammoth presence of Big Tech and social media in our lives.

I would like to support them to create a new way of relating to this technology/activity beyond the *status quo* that's more active and creative. Perhaps that could include creating new conversations among students and staff. Are there any questions or offers I could make to my students that could take us somewhere new?

Thank you,
Too Late to Make a Difference? NY, NY

Dear Too Late,

Thank you for writing to me and sharing your upset and despair. I'd like to help with that. Maybe if we do a little "unpacking" of your and your students' relationship (and its relationship to the *content* of the class, i.e., academic writing), we might discover something that could transform how it's going for all of you.

You seem dissatisfied with your role in the classroom conversation stemming from many of the students' research and writing about the negative mental health implications of social media. How I wish I had been a fly on the wall! For while you describe what the students said, you haven't said how you responded to them. What did you say? How did the conversation go?

Did you share with them any of what you're sharing now with me and our readers? If not, then that is one offer you can make that could possibly take you and your students somewhere new. The things you write in your letter—what you're struck by and concerned about (what you view as their passivity, for example)—these seem to me to be legitimate topics that could potentially make the conversations developmental intellectually and emotionally.

Introduce a "Becoming Curious Challenge." Offer them a "Performing Philosophy Challenge." For example, share your reaction to the "buzz words" and how come you call them that. Ask them if they ever thought about them in that way, or at all? Are they curious as to how come the buzz words upset you?

Invite them to play with psychological language and discover if and how it's different from other language (How is "I have anxiety" like "I have black hair"?). You might even invite them to ponder this: the negative mental health implications they identify with social media can be—and have been—said about most everything people do *when we're not on social media*! What do we make of that?

These are just a few suggestions off the top of my head, as they say. They're meant to re-*activate your creativity* in the face of what sounds, in your letter, like some painful moments of your own passivity.

Developmentally yours,
Lois

Trying to Be Perfect Is Exhausting!

Dear Developmentalist,

I work in a mentally stressful line of work; my mind is always working and churning, even outside work hours. I am good at managing this stress, but at times, it can become so much that my brain won't function.

And I am a perfectionist. I've learned to tone it down a bit over the years, but I have a fear of failing or messing up, particularly if the task is new to me. I will spend extra time working on it but hesitate before submitting it to my supervisor. Sometimes, I find it hard to get started with a task, but once I start, things do move forward.

On good days, I can get a lot done; but even then—and even though I acknowledge what I have achieved—I always think I could have gotten more done or been more consistent or productive.

I cannot change my line of work or change jobs, at least for now. (I do actually like my job and colleagues.) So, how do I get my brain to cooperate with me? How can I control it, overcome my fear, be able to start working and send my work to my supervisor without re-editing it ten times and stretching the deadline to its limits?

Thank you,
A tired perfectionist

Dear Tired Perfectionist,

Being a perfectionist sounds exhausting! And so, I welcome your letter and a chance to help you explore how it might be helping but also getting in the way of you creating the life you want. I can't tell from your letter whether you want to develop into less of a perfectionist or not. You say you've toned it down a bit, and maybe that's enough for you. If so, maybe the developmental step for you now is to create new ways to relate to your perfectionism.

But you're asking for help with your brain. You say it doesn't function or cooperate with you and you want to *control* it. How did you come to blame your brain? (I believe there's nothing—and nobody—to blame.) It sounds like you believe your brain is not only the source but also the solution to your fear of messing up or your hard time getting started on a task.

Our brains are involved in everything we do so, of course, they are playing a role here. But to relate to our brains in this way is, as far as I can tell, not very productive. Because we are so much more and far, far more complex than that! Your brain, after all, is in an environment that includes your body, the spaces in which you live your life, your society, culture, and history, and more. Your brain "works" with all of that, so separating it out in isolation greatly narrows what you have at your disposal to work on and play with to become less of a perfectionist—or at least to become less stressed by being one.

You say, but almost in passing, that you like your job and your colleagues. This is a great place to begin. It's something positive that could have an impact on the way that you carry out your job. So, I suggest that you spend a little more time thinking about it. I wonder what liking your job and colleagues looks and feels like for you. What kind of relationships do you have with colleagues? How do they see you? Have you spoken with them about your stress and perfectionism? How do they and your supervisor see this playing out in the job you do and in their relationships with you? Maybe you can begin to get to know yourself and them in new ways by creating possibilities to bring these kinds of questions into your conversations. After all, it is through others that we become ourselves.

Your job sounds demanding, but not nearly as demanding as you seem to be on yourself. I would think that it's your own demands that are making you tired. I hope that you can start making use of what you like and enjoy about your job and colleagues, for I think that might give you more energy.

Developmentally yours,
Lois

I'm the Goddess of Competition

Dear Lois,

Competition has been a major part of my life, and I don't think I'm alone in this. Particularly in America, it's everywhere! We live in a world organized by winners and losers.

We cheer a winning goal, watch contestants voted-off islands and trivia teams strike gold. Comparisons and superlatives are irresistible. We're captured by a "look at me" life!

Personally, I experienced competition from early in life, growing up with a brilliant and talented older sister. She easily commanded the lion's share of dinner time conversation, responding quickly to my father's questions on history, current events and philosophy. Later, my father insisted that I had the benefit of becoming scrappy and a fighter, and more capable by having had to fight for attention (i.e., self-improvement through competition!)

I like competitive games, and I like to play to win. I scope out the rules and success criteria for most anything I do—not only games—but in many aspects of life. I like to strategize and improve my approach to get better and win.

Still, I find the domination of this form of human activity exhausting even as it is thrilling and addictive. I'm getting tired of comparing myself and of being viewed and judged and compared to others. It feels demeaning, boring and non-developmental. Some of my relationships seem to be trapped in an endless and pointless competition/comparison game. The stuck-ness is frustrating.

Finally, I'm a parent and I don't want to pass along this one-track competition emotional roller coaster to my child, who already has internalized competition by way of school sports, grades and via social media.

Is there a developmental way to play with competition and to function differently in this world riveted on winners and losers?

Signed,
Free Your Time

Dear Free Your Time,

Is there anyone who doesn't have a love/hate relationship with competition? I doubt it. So, if it's any consolation, you're in good company! You're probably rare, though, in wondering if there's anything developmental we can do with competition. I imagine most people reading this don't know they can ask such a question but will be so glad that you did, because your question invites us all to look at competition in a new way.

So when you ask, "Is there a developmental way to play with competition and to function differently in this world riveted on winners and losers?" I think you're already on a developmental path. As I see and experience it, developing is a transforming of *what is* in such a way that it becomes what it "is" AND something else.

Becoming a "languager" (a speaker, a signer perhaps, a writer, a reader, and a maker of meaning) of a second language, for example, both adds something new AND transforms your language-ing in your first language—both of which qualitatively transform your relationship with others, with language and with yourself.

I agree that "we live in a world organized by winners and losers." And yet, I invite you to take another look at the world we live in, for that is not all there is. Visit a park. Watch some kids build a snowman. Eavesdrop on two strangers making small talk. What else do you see? Make a list.

Yes, competition seems to be everywhere, but being everywhere doesn't have to mean it's all-consuming and smothering (not your word, but mine for how you seem to feel). To use a theatre image, competition may well be the name of the play that, like it or not, we're all characters in—but it's not the only show in town. You are (can be) a character in another play and another and another and another. Living is like that. We often feel trapped by what we see and feel and how we move through the world, as if we were cast in a play we didn't audition for and don't want to be in.

I say, work on developing your character in "the competition play!" Maybe you're the one who wildly cheers for everyone else or conducts everyone in a "Congratulations!" orchestra. Or maybe you're "The Goddess of Competition" and give an acceptance speech to an adoring crowd. No matter what they are, your interventions are bound to put some unexpected plot twists into the competition play.

At the same time, Free, work on continuing to create and perform in all the other plays of your life, those not organized into winners and losers. Make a list of them. You'll probably still have a love/hate relationship to competition. But *performing this relationship with intention* will be transformative. You won't be free, but I do believe it might "free your time."

Developmentally Yours,
Lois

CHAPTER 11
WHAT A WORLD!

I'm an Emotional Mess in a Seriously Messed-Up World

Dear Developmentalist,

Lately I've been going through a bit of a shift in thinking about how and who I want to be in the world. Or perhaps I've been settling into who I have become. Whatever this is, it's making me uneasy, and I'm emotionally all over the place!

I am so glad to live my life in community. I love the work I do as an activist. And yet, I want more. Even when things are "going great," I'm vulnerable to self-diagnosing and self-blaming; I have so many harsh judgments about myself. I think this stunts my growth and ability to embrace and give all that I have.

I recently came across this quote from Epictetus: "He is a wise man who does not grieve for things which he has not but rejoices for those which he has." I want to rejoice and relax. But I find that close to impossible.

I see how much I rile myself up. I get so angry, fearful, and upset about the state of the world: the war in the Ukraine, earthquakes in Turkey and Syria, war in the Middle East, to name a few. It's all so very heartbreaking. I send money but that doesn't seem like enough. The mental health crisis, violence, poverty, corruption, the erosion of democracy, the persistence of racism and antisemitism, all impact me greatly. I know I am not alone in this!

I'd love some guidance on how I might allow myself to be in the world without so much strife. I don't know how to have all of what I feel living in our world without judging and diagnosing myself. And at

DOI: 10.4324/9781003528364-13

the same time, I am quite aware that I'm responding to the world. What would it be like to allow myself to feel what I feel without the harsh voice that insists that "something must be wrong with me"?

With gratitude,
Marni

Dear Marni,

Thank you for writing—you sure got me riled up! And, I suspect, many of our readers too.

Let's begin at the end of your letter, where you say that you want to rid yourself of the harsh voice that insists that "something must be wrong with me." Again, I suspect many of our readers would like nothing more than to silence that voice. My advice? Don't. Don't try. It just increases your pain and alienation.

How could there *not* be anything wrong with you? Since we are (all of us—no matter our politics, aspirations, and stress levels) *in and of this world*. We can't *not* respond to it. There's so much terribly wrong with the world, how could there not be anything wrong with you? Or me? Or anyone?

Martin Luther King, Jr. urged us to never adjust to injustice and "man's inhumanity to man" (*sic*)—and to be proud to be *maladjusted*. It sounds like you are—that you embrace being maladjusted to the ills of the world and how you work as an activist to do away with or at least lessen them. Perhaps you're morally, intellectually, and societally committed to being maladjusted, but you hedge on your embrace of being emotionally maladjusted.

You say, Marni, that you have a lot in your life, but you "want more." I suspect you really want "other"—specifically, *to be other*. Isn't that what self-diagnosing and self-blaming are all about? ("I hate the way I am!")

My advice? Embrace your emotional maladjustment and grow from there. You might develop into someone who can rile herself up and rest at the same time!

Developmentally yours,
Lois

My Voice Is Not Welcome — Right or Left

Dear Lois,

I live in a bedroom community that is polarized politically. And while the demographics are shifting, people who hold extreme views, either conservative or liberal (with which I am aligned politically) are vocal and local elections have been ugly.

There is an *us-vs.-them* feel to it all, and at the heart of most of the issues—if you can look past the rhetoric and inflammatory statements—is *identity*. Unfortunately, everything about how we school our kids is filled with hot button issues and leaves students caught in the middle.

There are threats and trash talking from both sides as we grapple with community issues. As someone who cares deeply about my community and wants to make a difference, I am struggling to figure out how to do that. My engagement with the liberal-leaning political group has left me feeling overwhelmed by a competition around proving how liberal we are. There's a hefty dose of sanctimony and an unwillingness to see grey areas or cultivate empathy.

My personal connections to people on the conservative side have left me feeling vulnerable. I am a single, self-employed parent with a business in town and have been reluctant to take a public stand after receiving some threatening messages, especially since I do not agree with a perpetuation of closed mindedness.

My heart hurts because I see people on both "sides" who could make change if they would only work together. But they seem unwilling to engage in dialogue, or to appreciate the complexities of a situation, or to accept that they might be wrong. I have limited resources of time and money; I am concerned about angering those who have been willing to point fingers and make threats—and I still want to help start a dialogue. I have no idea how. Do you have any ideas?

Signed,
Stuck Left-of-Middle

Dear Stuck,

I so appreciate your heartfelt letter that speaks to something causing great pain for so many of us who live in the United States (and, sadly, many other nation states). My guess is that most people want to do something about it, as you do, and they are as stuck as you are. Alongside the anger and disappointment toward fellow citizens for their inflammatory ways of speaking and unwillingness to give up their knowing stance, frustration at an overall cultural environment in which you must have one of two political identities, there is the real fear of retaliation, being ostracized or worse. It's hard to be creative, see new possibilities, and take risks in such a mass emotional state!

Still and all, you believe that we can do better, that people on both sides in your community can come together to make change. I so agree with you!

The question, of course, is how. While I have no answer—*you all will have to create it*—I do have some direction for changing how you see yourself and your role in this very bad play your community is creating. It is a direction that might activate you and others to try some new ways of relating.

You're probably right that at the heart of most of the contentious issues is identity. You must be left or right. You must be conservative or liberal when it comes to children and schooling. And so on.

What I wonder about, though, is *your* identity. I wonder if you think you're not playing that game in wanting to bring people together. I love that intention, but not the position you have placed yourself in—the identity you've assumed—i.e., *being in the middle.* Aren't you unknowingly accepting the either-or, this-or-that framework by creating another identity within it? And might this "place" be a source of stuckness?

Let's imagine another "place" you might be. Perhaps it's another identity, or another kind of identity. I don't think you're in the middle. I think you are *left out.* Your desire for people to change the toxic discourse, to create dialogue, to work together to make change in the community—all this is left out of how things are now. You, and others like you, are left out.

How you might go forward is to be proud of being left out rather than being victimized by being in the middle and to take action grounded in this pride.

It will not be easy! But you have two things going for you. One is the history of your community. In the past and even now, I am sure there is much that's been accomplished without toxicity. What things do people have in common? (Loving nature? Playing outdoors? Local rituals and celebrations?) What do they agree on? What are they proud of accomplishing together? Find ways to draw on those things, tell stories about them, build with them, play with them. Maybe you can invite people to make meals/picnics/bake sales together, to sing or read or write poetry together—these fun and politically neutral activities, even if just a couple of people participate, can start the ball rolling. They will have created something new together. Maybe they'll do it again.

The second thing you have going for you is the many projects and associations that are working for the same goal. You can draw confidence, inspiration, and practical ideas from them. I've made a list of resources for you to check out. While they are less creative and playful than I would like, they are all trying something new.

Living Room Conversations
Moral Courage
National Coalition for Dialogue and Deliberation
Uncomfortable Independent Conversations
Organizations Transforming Polarization and Division

In a nutshell, my advice to you is—Don't let your community keep you out!

Developmentally yours,
Lois

Caste, Class, and Religion: How Can We Still Be Friends?

Dear Lois,

We hear the constant admonitions: "The poor deserve their poverty!" "To the victor goes the spoils." "There's only one God—mine—and for the non-believers—cheat them, maim them … anything goes!" "The people elect the government they deserve!" And so on. Most of my conversations seem to end in damnation of the other (the enemy).

My personal story: Abdul, David and I went to the same middle school. Abdul and David lived in hutments (a hut encampment) that contained our school and living quarters. Neither of them made it to high school. Both of them were god-fearing, had faith, saw life as a test. They went from one menial job to another, and ultimately rose to a comfortable position and income, all thanks to the rising prosperity in India. Abdul and David's journeys are exemplary success stories. And yet now, as a highly educated engineer who has spent 20-some years studying and working abroad, the only reason I am still able to have any conversation with them is because we enjoy reminiscing about "good" experiences: sharing lunch, playing games, helping each other to study.

The historical (Indian) story: India's cultural underpinnings—its religious intertwining of Islam, Christianity and Hinduism—creates a bewildering story. Christianity came with Capitalism and Colonialism. Left-leaning, secular intellectuals are primarily anti-Hindu, and proclaim their secular ideals as progressive. The endemic corruption of state and local governments, their posture of appeasement, has ushered in a new variety of neo-colonialism.

Abdul, David and I, and millions of others in India, are witness to crimes and excesses of those who are rich and/or in power. Just today, a juvenile was arrested after she tweeted against an elected official. She won't be able to access public education, resources or even get a job in India. We accommodate injustice and corruption and the actions of a Hindu-reigning political class by leaning on our religious "faith" and the "Golden Rule."

Mere mention of Abdul or David (who are not Hindu and not from well-to-do, middle-class families) to my other Hindu friends can drive them nuts. Any conversations about the many fault lines in modern India (it's unsafe to speak across religious lines in social media!) produce a lot of name-calling, heartache and retreat into our inner "escape spaces."

Lois, I want to hear your thoughts on how we—citizens of this modern India—can talk more honestly about our fears, our community's expectations and what kind of a world we want to live in?

Regards,
Mahesh, Delhi, India

Dear Mahesh,

Thank you for sharing the anguish you feel about some of the divisions that get in the way of you and your fellow "citizens of modern India" discovering and creating the kind of world you want to live in. While "caste, class and gods" are, as you say, major identities dividing India's people, this same kind of anguish goes beyond political-cultural histories and national borders. Indeed, identity politics and its destruction of human life and spirit is a global condition. And so, your question—"How can we go on with these divisions?"—could be asked by every one of us, no matter where we are.

But let's begin with your story—actually, your two stories—one of which you identify as your "personal story" and the other as "the historical (Indian) story." That is so interesting to me!! Maybe if we explore the two stories and their relationship to each other we can discover ways to go on.

Your (personal) story includes David and Abdul, friends from middle school who you are still occasionally in touch with. Because of the deep political, cultural and religious divisions in India that also divide the three of you, you write that "the only reason, I am still able to have any conversation with them is because we enjoy reminiscing about 'good' experiences: sharing lunch, playing games, helping each other to study." I understand you to be saying that this shared history is how come you three can talk with each other. If that's the case, then your conversations could be so much richer and more varied. Because you three share so much more!

Everything you write in your historical (India) story is part of your, David's and Abdul's shared history—as is all that came before and continues in this extended moment of "a new variety of neo-colonialism"—including religious wars, British rule, partition, independence, corruption and, of course, the COVID pandemic. Recognizing that your personal story includes the history of India and its people (that is, it's something else the three of you share) gives you three a lot more to talk about than your good experiences together in middle school. I'm sure you could speak for hours on the experience and impact on each of you, in the past and today, of so many moments in and aspects of Indian history and culture. That's one way to "go on with these divisions."

Now it's time to return to that initial question. I think there's a more active, or activistic, question than how can we go on. And you already asked it! Right at the end of your letter, you ask, "how can we citizens of this modern India talk more honestly about our fears, our community's expectations and what kind of a world we want to live in?"

When I look at your two questions side by side, I think you must be saying something like this: "These divisions exist, and so we have no choice but to go on with them." But we do have some choice in *how* we do that. Can we go on with more honesty? Can we talk more openly of our hopes and fears and dreams? I love this question and the challenge of how to make it happen. Because it's not pretending the divisions don't exist or even trying to eliminate them. Rather, it's "building with what we have" (the very basis of development and growth) and making something new out of it. If what you have is deep divisions, then what you have to build with has to include them. And that goes for you, David and Abdul, all of India, and all of humanity.

Developmentally yours,
Lois

Roe v. Wade: How Can I Not See You as the Enemy?

Dear Lois,

Is it the end of Roe v. Wade? What does it mean? On my social media feed, it looks like this: Our god is bigger! (The crowd cheers in front of a big phallic statue.) Boohoo! I'm so angry! 69% of Americans want to keep Row v. Wade! Yaaay! Human life prevails! This is the opportunity for women to help that embryonic life become a productive human being! Fuck you Jean, you pro-lifer! I'm for Jane, I'm for Becky, I'm for Annie! Fuck you, you pro-choicers! Women's role is to reproduce! So how do we build with this crap?

Since yesterday, I have been speechless, sad and conflicted. I am a woman and can't understand how abortion could not be considered a "liberty." As a French woman, I have a hard time understanding the US Constitution and the particular rules of the laws of the land. As a daughter of a doctor, as a mother of a daughter, I am thinking of our women's history.

You might say: what does understanding have to do with anything? I don't know. I have a hard time. I am angry. I see the crazy, noisy pro/against game that is organized and presented to us and that produces anger, anger, and more anger and division. And I'm angry that we are fighting with each other.

I am tired of the pro-against game, not because I don't have a very big opinion (Oh, Liberté, Cherie!), not because I don't believe that my values are right (we are organized that way), but because I come to think that the game does not work. We are bad at this game.

So, how do we produce development? How can we organize cultural development with all the pain that goes with it?

Thank you for your thoughts and for this space, Lois!
A.H., Paris to Brooklyn, New York

Dear A.H.,

I appreciate you reaching out and sharing your pain and anger and sadness with me and our readers. I think it might be better to do so here than on social media platforms. As you say, they are perpetuators of "the crazy, noisy pro/against game"—and that game produces more anger and pain and sadness.

I can feel your passionate concern with the lives of women and girls and your desire that not just they—but all people—have the opportunity to develop. And that developing will, you and I hope, create something other than the pro/against game.

I am wondering, and invite you to wonder along with me, what you mean by "we are bad at this game." I wonder who the "we" is. I wonder what being bad at it looks like to you. I wonder what it would look like to you if we were good at it.

I wonder about these things because, to me, it's the game that's bad—regardless of how well or badly we (and here I mean everyone) play it. Perhaps this is what you mean also. I venture to guess that most of the players are as angry as you are. If so, then it's the game, not the players, that needs changing.

And who's to do the changing? The players! "Oh no," you lament! "These people (on both sides) who spew insults, who demean and demonize each other—they're who we have to count on to change the game?" A.H., I believe so. I think that's what's so hard, so painful, and so scary about all the horrors in the world. They will stop if people create something other than horror.

The current game is indeed horrible. It is horribly distortive; it makes human sociality, human creativity, human compassion and human humility exceedingly hard to see. But they are still there. How do we make them manifest? How do we create great performances? We cannot know. We might not even be able to imagine its possibility. No matter. We can, so far as we are able, create its possibility.

Developmentally yours,
Lois

As a Young Asian Woman, I Don't See Myself as a Leader

Dear Developmentalist,

I'm in a social therapeutic coaching group where part of our work has been to explore who we are in the world, our racial, ethnic/cultural backgrounds, socioeconomic status, the privilege that comes with all of that, and how we can break out of these identities and stereotypes. I've shared my history as a Japanese national, living in the US, building my career, and the hardness of all that at this moment.

I recently talked to the group about how I felt I'd lost my passion and zest for life, how I was feeling a bit flat—not quite like "myself." My career is in transition, I'm working to establish myself as an independent artist after having worked for another artist for years. I've waited years on pins and needles for an unconditional green card that would allow me to stay and work in the US. I hadn't been able to go home to Japan to visit my family during the pandemic because of travel restrictions. And I was frightened and angered by the rise in Asian/American hate crime all around us. I had been standing on extremely unstable ground for so long. It was really hard. This spring, I was finally able to visit Japan with my husband—my unconditional green card in hand! And while I felt a weight and darkness slowly lifting, much of the heaviness and hardness remain. I'm still hypervigilant each time I leave my apartment. And I still feel alarmed by COVID.

As I opened this up with my group, one of my group members said that she still feels and sees my fire. Those words brought tears to my eyes, since I haven't felt that fire for so long. The group also shared their experience of me as a leader in our group. They talked about how loving I was of them, a love that looks a lot of ways, including sometimes like anger. Hearing them tell me about my "leadership" felt hard. A "Japanese woman in her thirties" like me is not the "right" kind of person to be a "leader." Someone who's searching for a career path *shouldn't* be regarded as a person who "leads." But in considering other ways we talked about what it means to be a leader (e.g., being responsible, being accountable, taking our relationships seriously) and what it means to love, I felt it was freeing. And yet, it's still hard to let how they see me land.

How can I get better at being open to and receiving what the group is giving me? What do I do with the conflict I'm feeling being related to as a leader?

Sincerely,

M.S., San Francisco, California

Dear M.S.,

First of all, thank you for this honest and open letter. As I read it, I feel—like your group does—that I am in the presence of a loving person. It sounds like your letter is continuing the group's exploration of the complexity not only of who you all are (and are becoming) but also what this group activity produces, developmentally speaking.

It sounds to me like it's produced some surprises for you. "You see my fire and passion?" "Me, a leader?" I am curious, and I hope you are too, to explore the disconnect between your view of you and the group's view of you. For example, one of the ways you see yourself is as "a Japanese woman in her thirties." I wonder if the group even sees you that way and, if they do, I'm sure that description doesn't have the heavy cultural meaning that it does for you.

Culture shapes us, gives us identities and norms and expectations, and sanctions only certain ways to understand and experience and respond to our discontent with how "our" world is. If we don't conform to how we're told to feel given our identity, then we are not "really" Japanese, a woman, an artist, a leader, and so on.

The wonder of humans is that we can reshape all that. Countless times in history, culture—in the broad sense of how people live—has been transformed into a new cultural (political-economic-intellectual-ethical-psychological)—norm. Masses of people can do that together. Families can do that together. Groups of all sizes and shapes can do that together. And it's always a struggle, not only with others but with ourselves.

To me, what's profoundly important to realize about this social process of creating something new culturally is that the old "stuff" doesn't go away. It lingers. It co-exists with the new. I don't believe that we can ever completely "break out" of identities and stereotypes and the emotions that they produce. What we can do is create new emotions, new ways to feel about being who we're told we are, even as we become other. The Japanese woman in her thirties who is not a leader will still be there. She just has to move over to make room for some new emotional and relational ways for you to be you.

Developmentally yours,
Lois

How Do I Say "No" When I Have Nothing to Give?

Good Morning! Thanks a lot for sharing all this concerning development, which I find very interesting.

I have a question for you: Why is it sometimes very hard to say, "I
hear you asking for something from me, but I don't have what you are
asking for. I don't have it to give you."

To me, that response is different from simply saying "no," which
implies that I *could* give you what you're asking for, but I don't want to
and refuse to.

Sometimes people assume you could say yes to their requests, that
you have the means or resources. But by making this assumption, they
are behaving like kids thinking that others (like their parents) have all
the power.

Would be interested to hear your thoughts.

Very best,
H.H., Niamey, Niger

Dear H.H.,

I am so appreciative that you follow this column and find what I
have to say as the developmentalist interesting—so thank you!

Responding to people asking us for something is very common
and very complicated. You're certainly not alone in finding it challenging, and so it's great that you brought it up here.

As you point out: it's not so easy to say no! It seems that for you,
it's hardest to say no when you don't have it to give. For others,
saying no when you have it to give (but don't want to) might well
be harder.

I'm very glad that in your letter you brought up *assumptions*.
Everyone has them a million times a day. We can't stop making
assumptions. But we can *make use* of the ones we and others
make!

To make developmental use of our and others' assumptions, I
think we first have to recognize them in our interactions—we have
to appreciate how *interpretive* they are and how distancing they
can be. After all, assumptions come from and rely upon particular

interpretations we make about, or particular meaning we give to, what someone does.

So, for example, you say, "Sometimes people assume that you could say yes—that you have the means or resources to do so. But by making this assumption, they are behaving like kids thinking that others (like their parents) have all the power."

Can you see that you are interpreting *their* behavior and giving some underlying meaning to *their* ask of you? And, just as important, do you recognize *your own* assumptions in doing so?

My advice is to begin to practice recognizing assumptions—your own first and foremost. And then, explore them, preferably socially. In the case of being asked for something, challenge your assumptions—about what you're being asked for, about the relationship you have with the person who is asking, and about how you feel being asked by this particular person.

Keep going! Do you know each other? Like each other? What is your relationship? Are you flattered by the request? Are you annoyed? Are you ashamed?

Can you imagine a conversation in which you both share some assumptions and play around with these questions? If you can, then try it! It could turn out to be developmental for both of you and, of course, for your relationship.

Developmentally yours,
Lois

How Do I Deal with the Stigma of Homelessness?

Dear Lois,

The stigma of homelessness is intractable. The press helps spread negative ideas on those experiencing homelessness, making a remedy more difficult. Consequently, the poor, including working poor, have strained relationships, personal and otherwise, thanks to misperceptions. Solving problems is more difficult with those around you who want to avoid you. There is even the threat and danger of violence.

What does a developmentalist say about stigma, public psychosis and social isolation?

Philip

Dear Philip,

Thank you for your letter. You have raised questions about topics I too care deeply about—stigma, public psychosis and social isolation. I do need to add homelessness itself, however, as I believe it is one of the cruelest manifestations of the increasing disregard of human life in our times.

What can be done? As a reader of my column, you won't be surprised that I believe that development is the cure for homelessness and the other sicknesses you mention. As we humans are currently organized—and I mean that in every way—into seeing us vs them, into a pathetically limited range of "accepted" emotions, into adaptation to ever more deranged normalcy, into blame and shame, into mass hopelessness—there is next to no chance of transforming how we live together. Stigma against those who have no home is "othering" of the worst sort. I would say it is a form of public psychosis. The resulting social isolation is fed by the blame and shame world view, another form of public psychosis.

In such a cultural and economic environment, it is not easy to embrace the fact that we all live together on this planet. While there is a small proportion of the world's people who benefit greatly from how we are currently organized to live together, I have no doubt that the vast majority are desperately unhappy with the arrangement. But their (our) development—our capacity to collectively create hope and perform new possibilities, to transform how we see and think and feel—is being stopped by so many institutions in so many ways.

As I mean it, development is the activity of transforming our emotionality, our morality and our cognitive capacities, of creating qualitatively new and different ways of living together on this planet. How do we do that collectively, as a mass movement?

Way back in 1967, Dr. Martin Luther King, Jr. showed us the way. Turning the psychological notion of maladjustment on its head, he called upon the world's people to form a new organization, the International Society for the Advancement of Creative Maladjustment. "And through such creative maladjustment," King said, "we may be able to emerge from the bleak and desolate midnight of man's inhumanity to man, into the bright and glittering daybreak of freedom and justice."

House or unhoused, it is the creatively maladjusted among us (like you, Philip) who must create possibilities.

Developmentally yours,
Lois

Death. War. Sickness. My Life Is a Mess

Dear Lois,

It's been a rough 6 months. My father died about 6 months ago. I had a pretty complicated relationship with him—bad and good. He died the way he lived—with the good and bad there. To the extent I had hopes he would change, his death is forcing me to really let go of those hopes. It's sad.

As a Jewish person, I used to be a Zionist but haven't been for a number of years. Some of my closest friends and family are Zionists. Listening to people whom I love and respect justify genocide (or not talking about what's happening in Israel and Palestine) breaks my heart a little more every day. I feel ashamed. I don't feel that I am doing enough to help, and I'm not even sure that the things I do know how to do would actually help.

And sickness: I am at increased risk of serious illness if I get Covid. So, I have been very cautious. I learned that I do best with managing chronic illness when there is a lot of room to experiment and for admitting that there is a lot we don't know about how sickness works. But I am really struggling to keep finding ways to do this when it comes to Covid. And that's scary and frustrating.

To top it off, somehow, I lost my wallet and keys. I've never done that in my life! I'm feeling that maybe at a time when so many things are screwed up and impossible, I should feel grateful for having found a new way to screw up!

Signed,
Ugh

Dear Ugh,

I'm all for finding new ways to screw up! Seriously, it can help to put what you think of as your old screw ups in a new light. For starters, maybe it's not you that's screwed up. Maybe it's the world. I'm glad you shared your sadness, shame, fear, and frustration. These feelings sound to me like reactions to a screwed-up world. And for you over these past six months, they've taken a toll. Maybe thinking through them with me can create some new ways to feel or, at least, make some room for new feelings in the (hopefully) near future.

I wonder about your sadness. No matter how good or bad the relationship, how close or distant, how smooth or rocky, the death of a parent is usually experienced as a loss. My parents died many years ago and while it was sad, I'm not sure I experienced loss. I didn't *lose* my relationship with them growing up. I didn't lose the ways in which they helped shape me. I didn't lose who they were. And I didn't lose who they could still be.

And so, my question is, *can we be sad without feeling loss?* As much as we wish people would change, we can't make it happen. It sounds like you were able to build something with your Dad when he was alive in spite of wishing he were different. I think that you can still do that, and I hope you give it a try. You deserve it!

I venture that sadness is also at play with the changed relationship you have with family and close friends over the horrific situation in Israel and Palestine. You say that you want to help but don't know how, and that you feel ashamed that you're not doing enough. If you mean the situation, there are many ways to voice your feelings and give aid. If you mean your family and friends, you might share with them how painful it is to see your close relationship with them changing so dramatically and ask if they want to talk about that and see if there's something different you can do together, given that you and they see things so differently.

I wonder what it's been looking like to struggle to access practices and support regarding Covid-19 precautions. Do you no longer have access to the information and professionals who were helping you? Can you get some help in finding new ones? In my experience, illness is something we tend to do privately, but it's also something people are very eager to help us with.

As for your wallet and keys, by now you've probably found or replaced them. Far from screwing up, it's amazing that you've never lost them before!

Developmentally yours,
Lois

CHAPTER 12
SEARCH FOR METHOD

Do We Need Therapist–Patient Boundaries?

Dear Lois,

I recently watched a popular miniseries, *The Shrink Next Door*, with Paul Rudd playing New York psychiatrist Ike Herschkopf and Will Ferrell playing his patient, Marty Markowitz, and based on a true New York story. Just last year, the NY State Dept. of Health revoked Herschkopf's medical license after Markowitz brought complaints of abuse. The hearing committee cited "professional lapses … including gross negligence, incompetence, exercising undue influence, fraudulent practice and moral unfitness." I was conflicted and upset by the series. It's a worst-case saga of therapy gone bad and trust being broken. The show reinforces the "picture" that patients are fundamentally vulnerable and that we need protection from predators like Dr. Ike. There's no room for reflection … on therapy and friendship—on abuse—on vulnerability—on the role of the state. It's black and white. Marty is portrayed as indecisive, approval-seeking, lonely and socially awkward. He lets Ike take over the family business, embezzle his fortune, and move into his summer home in South Hampton. Marty only makes a move to end therapy and their friendship (after 27 years) when Ike leaves him alone after a frightening surgery, and lets his beloved goldfish die while Marty's laid up in the hospital. Critics (Bloomberg, *TIME*, *The NY Times*) were in agreement that Dr. Ike deserved his punishment after crossing the proper professional boundaries: doing his sessions while taking walks outdoors; mingling with patients at pool parties; setting up a charitable foundation to siphon-off Marty's life savings; and stepping in to control

DOI: 10.4324/9781003528364-14

the Markowitz family's multi-million-dollar business. Ike was not a good guy, to say the least. He hurt and abused Marty. But at the same time, in my work as a social therapy client for many years and as a developmentalist, I also believe that clients should not be cast as victims, whom the state needs to protect. I'm writing to you, because you have publicly challenged the APA on their authoritarian rules about "professional boundaries" in psychotherapy. And with these questions on my mind, I'm writing to you to see if we can further explore.

Sincerely,
J.W./New York

Dear J.W.,

Wow! There's already enough bad psychology and psychotherapy in film and on TV without a series devoted to it. To be fair, I haven't seen *The Shrink Next Door* so I can't comment on the quality or value of the therapy.

You ask for my thoughts as someone who has challenged the American Psychological Association (APA) for its rules on professional ethics—in particular, the standards it has set for what constitutes a violation of professional boundaries. (Note that in addition to the APA, associations of social work, counseling, psychotherapy, etc. have similar guidelines.) These standards purportedly protect the client from harm. From your account of what transpired in the TV series, Marty was clearly harmed by Ike taking advantage of him in many ways. Also from your account, I would agree that Marty was portrayed as a victim.

More to the point, however, is that he is understood to be a victim of a particular kind. No longer just a regular guy capable of being charmed and manipulated, as most of us are, he is now specifically and especially vulnerable by virtue of being in therapy. It's this identity that I object to most strongly. Because along with whatever DSM diagnosis clients get from therapists, they both now have this added identity to deal with. Part of what reinforces the victimized vulnerable identity is being treated as an isolated individual with an individual "problem," which is the basis and unit of mainstream psychology and psychotherapy and psychiatry.

With that out of the way, let's get to some other matters. Like relationships and development. Did Marty have friends? Family? Did he talk with them? Did he have a life? And Ike? Did he have colleagues or a supervisor he spoke with about his clients? Was Marty and Ike's relationship developmental for either of them at any point? Did Marty grow emotionally/socially in it?

And finally, we do have to ask, did Ike do anything illegal? If so, he should be subject to the laws of the legal system.

Developmentally yours,
Lois

I Lead a Group with Boys Who Live in a Virtual Game Land. How Do I Help?

Dear Developmentalist,

I am a coach and counselor. I see mostly young people in individual and group therapy. The boys in one of my groups talk non-stop about the VR (virtual reality) games they're into—the characters, strategy, weapons of choice, etc., etc. I try to be supportive and don't shut them down. But, still, it's a lot of what they bring to the group. It looks to me like they are excited to enter a world where you can (re)invent yourself and become anybody you want to be. A short, skinny kid can be big and powerful, and no one is the wiser. You can destroy your opponent, but when the game's over, nobody's hurt.

I feel conflicted. I want to be supportive, but I'm also very concerned to not leave them dangling in a fantasy world.

The kids are having fun playing games and talking about the games. But they are also having difficulty in many social situations and in their classrooms. They have trouble making friends. They get into fights. They act spaced out. They won't respond directly to questions and want to get back on their phones. Their parents tell me that some of them are spending maybe 1/3 of their time in V-R gaming environments. I can't help but imagine that there is a relationship between their spending more time in virtual game-land and the challenges they face being with other kids in real life.

Am I overreacting? How can I help these kids live (and grow) in this uncharted territory?

Caring and Concerned

Dear Caring and Concerned,

Thanks for sharing your conflict and giving us a glimpse of one of your groups. It has aroused both my appreciation of your conflict and my curiosity! First off, what brought them to counseling in the first place? I assume it was their parents! But what did they want help with with their children? Perhaps it was their worry that their sons were spending too much time in virtual worlds. Perhaps it was the challenges their kids have with other boys. Do they, like you, think there is some relationship between the two?

The reason I wonder about what brought them to group is that it seems important that they have a supportive environment to talk about how they understand and feel about being there, what they think they're there for, and what they want to do there with each other and with you. I wonder if you've created that space with them. It seems to me that you need their participation in order to discover how to support them as they navigate/create their young lives. I don't think you can assume you know what would support them.

You mention that the non-stop talking about their lives in virtual reality is going on in one of your groups. I wonder about the other groups—how they're different and similar, how you are different and similar, etc. And I also wonder if there are girls in any of the groups.

Getting back to the boys' "two worlds" and how they might be related, I'd love for you to consider exploring that with the group—and doing so playfully. For example, you might ask, "If you and that boy you fight with were in (name of one of their virtual games), what would you do? What might happen?" And the reverse: "Let's pretend that (whatever is happening in the virtual game) it's happening on the school playground." I'm curious about whether inviting them to cross over and connect what they do and feel in these different "realities" might lead to some new kinds of conversations with the group—and perhaps some discoveries of what else is possible.

Let's make uncharted territory a space for potential growth!

Developmentally yours,
Lois

Where's My Path to Empowerment?

Dear Lois,

I'm interested in what you think about what personal development has to do with empowerment, as my background from childhood and some of my adulthood has been less than empowering.

I have trained in Transcendental Meditation, studied Zen, Mahayana and Tibetan Buddhism and Hinduism as growth practices. They help me connect with my inner self. Creative visualization, meditation, and other methodologies common to pop culture are helpful too. These practices of "turning inward" seem directly relevant to my development. And yet, I'm wondering if and how such practices can also be empowering? What tools do we have (or do we need) in this political climate to empower ourselves?

I believe that solutions can be created by small activist groups to help address broad government failures. And that action is important. Together we can imagine a better world. But community practices, and my personal growth, are just one small piece in a world of wild geopolitics and oppression. Does my/our empowerment matter?

Thank you so much for your input!

Sincerely,
K.B.D./US

Dear K.B.D.,

Your letter catches me at a perfect time, as I've been thinking about empowerment the last couple of weeks myself. So, thanks for inviting me to explore this with you.

Your questions center around empowerment—ways to create it and ways to counter efforts to disempower. You wonder what role "personal development" can play in empowering ourselves and others and how "methodologies common to pop culture" might be useful in this effort.

Big issues. Timely issues. All the more reason to discover what we and others mean by empowerment!

I don't like the term empowerment and for years I avoided using it. But it's such an everyday word now that it's just about impossible to avoid, and so you will occasionally hear me or read me using it.

My problem with empowerment? This may sound paradoxical, but I think that empowerment has little to do with power. And I'm fiercely concerned with power!

To empower or to be empowered is to be given or granted something (some say power, but I think they really mean authority or legitimacy) by others. These others are typically those in authority who have a measure of control over you, like parents (as you hinted was part of your own history) and bosses and teachers and officials and lawmakers. As I understand power, it's something that people themselves generate, create and use. No one can give it to you. It's just not that kind of thing.

And this leads me to point out another paradoxical feature of our current times. This might be oversimplifying, but doesn't it seem as if the more that empowerment is becoming a "good" thing, that it's something people want, the more power is becoming a "bad" thing, that people want to avoid? All kinds of identity groups, not to mention citizens in general, strive for empowerment and, in the same breath, want to avoid power (which has come to mean "those IN power").

With these paradoxes in mind, K.B.D., let's return to your questions. You ask about development and empowerment. I think the relationship can go both ways—individuals and groups can develop themselves politically and emotionally so as to be able to make use of being empowered by others; and those who have been empowered by others can invest that in further and continuous development. It won't always happen that way, but we need to move "being empowered" in that direction. And that direction is the exercising of power for the ongoing and continuous creating of development.

As for visualizations, meditations, and so many more wonderful human activities that are now commodified and packaged as empowerment tools, well, enough said! By all means, do them if you want! But not instrumentally. Not for empowerment. More in the spirit of the spiritual master of meditation a friend recently told me about, who said that meditation is good for nothing. He meant it as the highest compliment.

Finally, imagining together a better world? Within a developmental frame, imagining has to be in a constant dance with the material making of the better world.

Happy meditating, happy imagining, happy creating, K.B.D.!

Developmentally yours,
Lois

What Is Emotional Development?

Hi Lois!

Lately I've found myself in conversations where I'm being asked to tell people what emotional development is. I may have mentioned to them that I am a therapist, or I may have invited them to a class or a workshop. When I get this question, I say things like it's "creating new emotional responses, relating to people in new ways, learning how to have conversations, co-creating possibilities in your life, etc."

But the reality is, I am not good with examples. I know you've been talking about emotional development for years and would like to hear what your answer is!

Much Love,
Majo in Mexico

Dear Majo in Mexico,

I greatly appreciate your question and the circumstances in which it comes up for you. "Emotional development" is not the easiest conversation starter, that's for sure! First off, development isn't something people typically think about. And even when it does enter consciousness or conversation, people's connection to development invariably has to do with babies and little kids. And what of emotions? Aren't they a basic grouping of feelings inside us (like anger, love, jealousy, fear, and so on)? How could it be that emotions develop? Don't we just need to manage them?

This is some of what you're up against. It's no surprise, then, that you're likely to get a blank stare, a glazed-over look or—in the best cases—a sincere, "What does that mean?"

You're right that I've been talking about emotional development for years! And you know what? Every time it's different! I try never to tell people what emotional development is. (I actually try not to tell people anything beyond what time it is or how to get to Times Square.) *Telling* can be a real conversation stopper.

It sounds like you might be equating "telling" with "talking." But talking is vastly broader than telling! There are so many things we can do when we talk, so many things we can create with how others hear and don't hear us and how we hear and don't hear them, with how we and they look and move our eyes and mouths and hands and bodies. But if we are focusing on telling it (in the "right" way), we can miss all of that. We can forget that we're creating a conversation with someone.

A conversation is a relationship builder—the relationship between you, who you're speaking with, and whatever your topic is. A developmental conversation is always improvisational, requiring you to at least entertain the possibility that you don't have any idea what you're talking about until the conversation is created. That's where the meaning is.

With this in mind, let's return to emotional development. Looking at the things you say you say (in your "telling")—"creating new emotional responses, relating to people in new ways, learning how to have conversations, co-creating possibilities in your life, etc."—what do you see? Better yet, say them aloud. What do you hear? Whatever you hear, you can be sure it's not what others will hear. That's the beauty and challenge and paradox of making meaning! Engaging in this beauty and challenge and paradox together can be developmental—emotionally and otherwise.

My advice? Create conversations with others. Focus on the relationship, listen to and for offers, explore concepts and opinions and experiences together. This will make your problem of "not being good with examples" vanish.

Developmentally yours,
Lois

What's Belief Got to Do With It? Part 1

Dear Lois,

Let me present this question from a couple of sides. First, the most straight-on way. People say all the time, "I believe" or "I don't believe." I believe in good. I believe in evil. I believe in empathy. I don't believe in empathy. I believe in God. I don't believe in God. And lately I realize that those belief statements don't make me more curious about God or good or evil or empathy. They make me curious about BELIEVING. What's believing got to do with development? Coming to the question from another angle, for the last 6–8 months I have been participating in a program called NOOM. I would describe it as a cognitive behavioral program to help people learn new eating habits; you could call it a weight loss program. And it's been helpful for me. There are some things that you do every day in NOOM: you weigh yourself; you record your food … and (I just reviewed the very first lessons you get with NOOM and I realized) … you believe! Every day, you get a little lesson/reading on food, sleep, stress, the body, the brain—some of it annoying, some interesting. But in the VERY FIRST NOOM lessons, there is that statement, "I believe (I can do it)!" And so the question, What's belief got to do with it? What's "I believe" or "I don't believe" got to do with it? I could say more, but I don't want to fall into some silly psychological wormhole. I think this is a good start. This question does interest me.

Sincerely,
K.S./New York

Dear K.S.,

Thanks for writing. What a juicy offer you've made! I don't know about keeping you from falling into a wormhole—that's out of human control. But a rabbit hole? I'll do my best.

My advice is to continue philosophizing. I agree you've made a good start by "being curious about BELIEVING." What does it have to do with development, you ask. Or (on a more mundane level) with following the NOOM regimen.

To help you in your philosophical performance, I call upon one of my heroes, Ludwig Wittgenstein. He wasn't merely curious about such things as belief; he was rather obsessed. (A collection of notes he wrote at the end of his life, exploring certainty, doubt, truth and knowledge was published years later with the title *On Certainty*.) As far as Wittgenstein was concerned, all propositions, including those concerning certainty, belief, and so on, have no meaning in and of themselves, but only in context—they make sense in certain language-games, that is, in relation to what is going on, to what people are doing when they speak with each other, etc. In one language-game, "water" might be a desperate plea for a drink, and in another it might be an instruction to someone who's house sitting your plants.

So, one suggestion I have is that you look and listen in a new way. Try to see and hear the language-games that are giving rise to your curiosity. I think you'll discover that "I don't believe in evil" and NOOM's "I believe (I can do it)" are "moves" in two very different language-games. Look at what's happening when someone, says "I don't believe in evil." Are people arguing? Rationalizing? Persuading? What else? And with NOOM, saying/thinking "I believe (I can do it)" is part of the losing weight activity. And it doesn't depend on how you feel! It's part of the performance of becoming a person who can successfully lose weight. And it works, right?

Your interest in believing calls for a little more philosophizing. Such as, "Hmm, if 'I believe/don't believe' doesn't always mean the same thing, then maybe it doesn't have anything it corresponds to at all!" And if that does occur to you, Bravo! You're performing Wittgenstein (which is surely developmental!). Because one of Wittgenstein's great contributions was demolishing what's known as the correspondence theory of language—that there is something "in the world" that words refer to. Instead, he saw language as "an activity, a form of life."

Wittgenstein said, "You can fight, hope and even believe without believing scientifically." My friendly amendment, in keeping with language as activity, is "You can fight, hope and even believe without believing correspondently."

And so, What's believing got to do with development? I have no idea, but I suspect "everything" and "nothing" depending … What I do believe, though, is that performing philosophically—as you are—has everything to do with development.

Developmentally yours,
Lois

"Contextualizing Belief?" I Don't Get It. Part 2

Dear Lois,

I have read the question and response regarding belief and believing and something in your response puzzles me. Perhaps this concerns the "correspondence theory of language," which I feel hesitant to speak about as distant as I am from such study. In any case, I hear your statements about "water" quite differently than those about "belief." Whether "water" is used in a plea from a dying person or as a request to water the lawn, there is something we call water that has a physical existence in the world and takes the same form whether watering a lawn or hydrating a dying person. It feels and looks and tastes the same in both language games if those are language games.

Belief, however, is an idea and therefore does seem to fit what Wittgenstein says about meaning depending on the language game that the word, in this case an idea, is part of. In other words, I cannot see how the meaning of water varies in the way that the meaning of belief varies depending on the language game each word appears in.

Yes, "water" means something different to a homeowner and to a dying person but isn't the water in both cases the same? But belief has no existence outside of language and so necessarily will vary depending upon the language game it appears in. So I feel puzzled when I read your response because "water" and "belief" seem to be spoken of as comparable examples of meaning changing with the language game.

D.D., Atlanta, Georgia

Dear D.D.,

I'm so glad you had a follow-up question to my response to K.S. I'll try to help you with your puzzlement. As I read your letter, you think of "water" and "belief" as materially different from each other and therefore are puzzled by the way I seem to imply that they are comparable in deriving their meaning from when and how these words are used. You concede that the meaning of "water" and the meaning of "belief" can vary according to context, circumstance, language games, etc. But since, according to you, water has a physical existence in the world and belief doesn't exist outside of language, there's a problem with me comparing them.

Don't take offense, D.D., at what might seem like me quibbling, but I didn't present them as comparable examples of meaning changing with the language game. No comparison meant at all. Just trying to help K.S. appreciate that it's we human beings who create meaning by our activity, that creating meaning is a cultural practice, and that words do not have meaning independent of the activity of speaking/writing/singing, and so on. And that goes for "water" (if, indeed, "water is water," as you say—and which I doubt: think, for example, of the water in Flint, Michigan faucets and Rocky Mountain streams) or any other word or term that mistakenly is thought to correspond to a material entity. And it holds equally for "belief" or any other word or term that mistakenly is thought to correspond to a mental state.

As I see it, the developmental challenge (for us all) is not a decision to accept or not accept the correspondence theory, but the willingness to practice and perform seeing and speaking and listening in ways that don't depend on it.

I *believe* that you can, and I hope that you will!

Developmentally yours,
Lois

Thanks for Your Advice ... But It's Just Not Me

Dear Lois,

I think this is a developmentalist question. ... See what you think. I have a close friend who's helping me make some major changes in my life. I'm about to transition out of my current job, and I asked a friend for help on how to get the ball rolling as I "recreate" myself.

I'm very appreciative of her assistance, but there are some things she wants me to do that I'd rather not—including talking about and promoting myself in ways that I don't feel totally comfortable with (and that includes writing to you for advice). It's not me. Do I tell her that I'd rather not take her direction (I'm concerned about being hurtful or disappointing)? Or should I just go ahead and do what she says, even though I really don't want to?

Thanks.
Uncomfortable, Washington, DC

Dear Uncomfortable,

Thanks for your question, which, as the self-named Developmentalist, I can assure you is, indeed, a "developmentalist question"! Before we go there, let me just say how fortunate you are to have someone to talk through things at a time when you're making what sound like big moves in your life. So many people do this alone.

What interests me most in your letter is you saying, "It's not me." I invite you to explore this assertion with me. I think it might help you with your dilemma over how to respond to your friend. What is that feeling? You say that you're not comfortable with some of the things your friend wants you to do. I get that. But how does feeling uncomfortable become "not you?" And how is doing something you wouldn't ordinarily do (or wouldn't do "on your own") not you? What does that mean?

You might mean that you're not the kind of person who does that type of thing. But isn't that your friend's very point, especially now when you are making some major changes in your life? Maybe this is one of those major changes!

Developmentalists like me believe that being/doing/performing "other than who we are" ("not me") is how we develop and learn and see ourselves and others in new ways. All this to mean that, to me, if it feels "it's not me" there's a good chance it will be developmental for you to try it.

This is not to say you should follow your friend's advice. The way you pose the question—"Should I just go ahead and do what she says, even though I really don't want to"— suggests to me that you'd not only be doing something you don't want to do but that you weren't taking your friend's suggestion as an offer to build with but merely an instruction to follow. No matter how the suggestion was made to you, you can and should relate to it like an offer—one that you can choose to create with (rather than "follow"), or not. That should also take care of your worry of hurting or disappointing your friend if you don't take her direction. Because there's all kinds of ways to respond to her offer that don't involve you doing what she says.

My advice? Become more of, and other than, who you are. That's a great way to "recreate" yourself. One more thing. There's more to life than, "Should I do this OR that." Create more choices— avoid the "either-or" bind.

Developmentally yours,
Lois

A Really "Uncommon Dialogue" (Arf! Arf!)

Dino is one of my family's two dogs. He is now four, and he and six-year-old Louie have been the best of pals since we adopted Dino when he was a few months old and added him to our family. They are both loving and quirky and generally well-behaved. Dino has calmed down considerably from his hyper-puppyhood. With the help of two of his human friends, he wrote a letter to "The Developmentalist" when he was about a year and a half. Dino's letter and my response were performed as part of a presentation at the Association for Applied and Therapeutic Humor's virtual annual conference in 2022. Dino was played by Kate McGlynn (Katy Bee), and I played myself. My response below is summarized from that presentation.

Dear Developmentalist,

I am a small dog who lives with a very loving family in a small beach town on the tip of a very long island. I love the beach, I love my people, I love to play (my favorite thing to play with is a little stuffed dirty squirrel), I love my brother, who is a somewhat larger dog who my people say is Zen. They've never said that about me. Which makes sense. I am, what they call, a yapper, and I've heard people say my voice has got a very high pitch. Which is what I want to get help from you around—developmentally of course. I yap anytime I hear noises (which my people don't always hear), I yap when I am excited, or scared or if I hear something I don't recognize. And I get riled up and yap when I hear other dogs bark. Which is paradoxical. The dog's barking riles me up and my barking, apparently in response to that, riles up my people. Is there a developmental way of dealing with this paradox?

My people do not like my yapping. At all. They try all sorts of things to get me to stop. They even spend money on devices that don't work at all. They yell at me. Sometimes they pick me up and put me places. Lately, I am happy to say, they have tried quietly saying "quiet," which is a little effective, but not really. But it is more pleasant.

So back to the development question. How can I look at this? I don't think I can stop yapping or barking. It's not like I decide to do it, it just comes out of me. And then when I hear my own bark, I yap some more. But I love my people and I don't want them to be irritated or sad or mad. It seems we're all stuck. Which is why I am writing to you, because

I heard you help people create new possibilities. I don't know if you've ever helped a dog create new possibilities, but I would like to. I've been listening to some of my people who read your column out loud, and it seems somehow tied to relationality, whatever that is. Do you think my people and I and my brother who is Zen might create development together?

Love,
Worried and Yapping at the Beach

Dear Worried and Yapping (aka Dino),

I am so moved that you wrote me, Dino! (Please thank the humans who helped you write your letter.) I take your caring about relationality, and our relationship in particular, as an expression of your love for and understanding of me. And it makes me love you even more!

Perhaps I don't understand you so well. Sometimes I try to understand your yapping, but sometimes annoyance overtakes me and I just want you to stop. So maybe we both need to be more curious about the other. You might wonder how come your yapping bothers me. You might wonder how come your brother (who is Zen) doesn't yap. I already do wonder about the situations and things you yap at. Do they all create the same emotion for you or different ones? I wonder if we can create some ways to make these discoveries together.

Because, as you say, it's all about relationality. Dogs and humans have a very long history of creating relationality. Many say that this is based in our discoveries of the ways we needed each other. You protected us, and we fed you. You kept us warm, and we fed you. You let us teach you how to make our lives a bit easier (hunting with and for us) and how to listen to us, and we let you teach us what you knew from your superior hearing, sight, and sense of smell. Through centuries we built mutuality through creating relationality.

Let's keep that in mind, Dino. You say that your yaps "just come out" of you, so you don't think you can stop. Do you remember when you were a little puppy and you peed all over the house? And then you didn't. Your pee "just came out" of you, too, just like your yaps. But you learned to pee when and where we thought it appropriate. What possible reason could there be for your development in this area except relationality? It mattered to the relationship we were building. The same goes for yapping.

So, let's not worry anymore. Let's keep getting to know each other and creating who we're becoming.

Developmentally yours,
Lois

Figure 12.1 *Dino and Me*

Chapter 13
Experiential Impact (Reverberations)

Now that you've read these letters and my responses to them, you might be curious—as I was—how they landed with readers. In this chapter, you will find commentary from several letter writers and other readers. Some of these other readers are therapists, counselors, and coaches who have written to share the impact of the letters–responses on their work with clients.

Comments from Letter Writers and Other Readers

From Letter Writers

From Marni

I've written two letters to "The Developmentalist" in the space of several years. Now that a bit of time has passed, I appreciate how Lois's responses have helped me.

I wrote for the first time after having a horrific bout of Covid and feeling a bit *traumatized* ("I've Been Traumatized … But Then, Who Hasn't?" p. 25). My father was into psychoanalysis and would often tell my brother and me that we were "traumatized" by events throughout our upbringing (… with him, our parent!) It was a word I both grew up with and pooh-poohed. I felt traumatized by my Covid experience, yet I was annoyed by the overuse of it as a buzzword.

Given world events and political strife, writing to Lois and receiving her developmental advice helped me navigate out of emotional crisis. I had only been seeing/feeling *my* trauma and *my* pain. One of Lois' eye-opening responses was that nowadays, *trauma* is "…seen as living *inside an individual person*, physically and psychologically, which makes a lot of human atrocity hard to see and deal with socially, culturally and politically."

Off this, I began to ask new questions: How could I not be in crisis, given that the world is in crisis? What is a developmental way to go through this kind of personal/world crisis? How do I want to do that? And with whom? I was able to challenge some of my emotionally maladjusted assumptions and attitudes about taking antidepressants, for example, which have helped me so much. I found a way to developmentally deal with a traumatic life experience—by doing it "exploratorily"—thanks to "The Developmentalist."

In a second letter ("I'm an Emotional Mess in a Seriously Messed-Up World," p. 97). I asked for help with all the ways I can *rile myself up*. I questioned if it's possible to be in the world in a new way, without the harsh voice that insists that something is wrong with me.

I'm so grateful for Lois' advice to "embrace [my] emotional maladjustment and grow from there." I believe I have been kinder to myself in these moments that rile me up. How? For one, I know how upset and angry certain things will make me, and I've gotten much better at not looking at this or that video or social media post, or watching mainstream media coverage of war, violence, and politics. Nowadays, I slow myself down and question if I must have this or that conversation with this or that person if the topic or person is likely to rile me up. I am much more able to embrace my emotional maladjustment *as a strength*, not a problem.

Thank you.

From S.F.

I found Lois' response to my letter ("Is It Time to Retire from the Company I Founded?" p. 73) extremely helpful. I had taken to re-reading it from time to time and have learned new things from it along the way. It was helpful to see (again) in her response that I'm indeed a lucky man—that I have choices that most people do not have, and that I have privileges that the bulk of the world doesn't have.

What I found most immediately helpful was her challenge to a fixed notion of "retiring" (stay or go?) Her observation and question to me: "How many ways are there to retire?" was transformative. Deciding to retire is a very different activity than *creating how you would like to be*.

To continue to re-create who you are and who you are becoming is very different than choosing a this-or-a-that outcome.

I have come to further embrace Lois reminding me that there are endless possibilities when you embrace the creativity that lives in wondering about the HOW. And, it's frankly way more fun too!

Thank you!

From Margaret, Michigan

It made me nervous to write you, Lois, about my concerns ("I'm Panicked That I May Be Getting Dementia," p. 77), since my mother and, very recently, my sister died from the disease. At the same time, it calmed me down to get it all out there in my letter to you.

I had been quietly amassing a "dementia checkbox" list: I get angry sometimes (check!); I have to write myself reminder notes (check!); I forget things on occasion (check, check, check!) It's a string of proof-points I keep in my head. Lois, you, pointed out that many people can (and do) check-off the same list. I don't think this was you trying to "normalize" my checklist (whatever "normal" means these days). Rather, your challenge was about me *keeping these fears/observations (privately) in my head.*

Worrying about what's happening to me has become self-deprivational and boring. I've come to realize that boring myself is my comfort zone. I'm familiar with the lists, the self-diagnosis, the fear. What made me chuckle, though, was coming to ask myself: "Do I really want to be this boring to others?"

It's an ongoing exercise to invite friends to tell me how they think I am, as you advised. At one end, I'm not asking for an evaluation every time I see someone. On the other hand, I'm not staying silent about my concerns. I'm someplace in the middle.

Sometimes when my friends ask: "Don't you remember …?" it still bothers me. I have to flex my intimacy muscles and say to them with good humor: "When it comes to memory, I'm a little like that old Almond Joy (candy bar) jingle: 'Sometimes I feel like a nut; sometimes I don't!'"

From J.B.

I so-appreciate your developmental advice, Dr. Holzman. I'm glad to tell you: It worked! Soon after our correspondence ("I Can Be a Snob:

I Keep Myself Distant with My Big-City Judgments," p. 88), I read my note and your response to my family (dogs and cats included, of course) which they all found helpful. They eagerly offered support for me to try out another neighborly role/performance.

To kick it off, we began by playing a game we invented called *the judgment competition*. We took turns being over the top with judgments we have toward others; then we all laughed (the dogs and cats didn't actually laugh—they are a tough crowd!)

A few weeks later, we were hanging out on our front porch with a couple of friends, enjoying the summer weather, when a couple down the street started walking toward my house, walking their dog. I said to myself, "Hey, they are the perfect neighbors to creatively imitate. They are always friendly, open and kind. I can try that too!"

My usual performance would have been to half-wave at them while they walked by. I asked my family for support to do another performance right then and there. (I was nervous and conflicted about trying something new. Wouldn't it be easier to keep doing what I've always done?) My family said, "Go for it!" So as they got closer, I called over to them and invited them to come join us on our porch, saying "Hi! I would love for us to hang out together!" And to our delight, they came over, and we all had a lovely, engaging afternoon conversation, dogs, cats and all!

From "Free Your Time"

Dear Lois,

Your response to my letter ("I'm the Goddess of Competition," p. 94) was helpful as a way to enlarge a world I felt trapped in. It was a reminder that the competition game isn't the only show in town! It was a prescription to observe and note different environments, conditions and whatever it was in my surroundings that freed me up from being trapped in this game (or that game, or whichever game it was), and from seeing most situations in my life through the lens of win-or-lose.

It is a new game for me now to seek out and create activity with others where competition is not at the center and doesn't drive the emotional environment. And in seeking, I am also creating. And using the theater language you introduce, I'm inviting my fellow actors to create a new play.

Thank you for the direction!!

From Emilie K., New Jersey

I asked for help with getting annoyed by my dearest friends ("I Get Annoyed by Everyone!" p. 23).

In her response to me, Lois did not judge! She didn't convey, "Hey, let's look at what is wrong with you!" So I wanted to read on. She wrote: "It's not only you," and right away, I was open to reading her response. She identified the issue as an activity—and that too helped me feel engaged. She made my getting annoyed intriguing—an activity to be investigated—an activity that she and I could begin together.

She unpacked the issue, presenting a new way to investigate my emotionality around annoyance. Was I also feeling angry, disappointed, etc. etc.? She proposed continuing to look into the activity of becoming annoyed and suggested moves I could make—investigating, playing with, trying new performances, talking with others and creating meaning with the emotional activity of being annoyed.

She challenged my assumption that I was annoyed *because of* actions or words of the other. Challenging that view allowed me to own and experience my emotionality—to slow down and notice from what vantage point I was looking from and then be empowered to make a (different) conscious choice.

All of this was extremely helpful! In fact, the phenomenon of "being annoyed by everyone" has been totally transformed and exists in my life as one among many ordinary, complex emotions rather than a "triggered" response I cannot control. I talk with friends about it, and they know about my tendency to do/be annoyed and of my work to share this with them and try out other performances. I do think that new meaning is created, at least, new intimacy with my friends. And I laugh about it now!

This is a huge, lasting relief. It provided a way to look at and challenge other presumptive ways of experiencing and responding to what we see as *triggers* for bad behavior and empowered me to be open to these investigations into learned and presumptive, usually narrowing, ways of being. I think I am an easier person to be around and really feel closer to all my friends since writing and having followed "The Developmentalist's" advice.

Thanks, Lois, for helping pull back the blinds to expose new possible worlds and ways to live. What a precious gift!

From "Rambling"

Dear Lois,

Reflecting months later, our correspondence ("My Co-Workers Say I Talk Too Much," p. 81) helped me enter into a moment of reflection and observation in a workplace that I found challenging. It became clear to me that this small, family-like setting wasn't healthy for me. I think my rambling (talking too much) was an outgrowth of me trying to fit into a very limited space at an organization which was itself ambitiously trying to stretch and grow but was still at the beginning.

There simply wasn't space for me, as I am: creative, curious, and sometimes quite opinionated. I did get bigger there and quickly decided to move to another role in a different organization, despite wanting to earn a feather in my career cap by "sticking it out." I learned that sometimes learning is fast and that the world is large. There are environments where I can use my creativity, curiosity and my voice, and be welcomed, and where my listening can blossom into growth and development.

Thank you for being with me in this conversation, Lois!

From "Maybe You Can't Go Home Again"

Dear Developmentalist,

It's me ("Maybe You Can't Go Home Again," p. 68)—writing with appreciation of our correspondence which has "started to land" a year and a half later. ("Better late than never," as they say in the growth business!)

I'd written that, as an adult returning to my family's home in the US South after 40 years, I had been overcome with the "emotions of the past" (the subjectivity of yesteryear) and was really in miserable shape. You wrote back with a letter that at that time, I found to be inscrutable.

You said that there was "no home to go back to." There were no "emotions of the past" that could be touched off by a landmark or food or other excursions down memory lane (Marcel Proust notwithstanding!) That my emotional time travel was an illusion. And that actually what there was, was the entirety of (my) history—including the history of "traveling back," emotionally speaking, to my childhood and early 20s.

I read and re-read your letter to me and hit a blank. I recognized the words and phrases but had no idea what you were talking about. I know I didn't like it when you suggested that my emotional time travel, while miserable, was also self-indulgent.

I told anyone who'd listen about what you'd said—how I thought it was both mind-blowing and inscrutable. I'd read your letter out loud. Most of them listened politely. I'd get excited and more confounded. And that went on for a while.

Then this week, I made another trip to visit relatives in the South and (lo and behold!) discovered development. I wasn't looking down memory lane (at least 2/3 as much!). I was getting to know new people in an old place—doing some new things with them, going swimming, playing poker, working on a health regime, talking politics, learning their way of slowing down and relaxing—some of which I could bring home to my city life.

I took a long walk on the beautiful beach, and was quite excited to find that it was ME walking down the beach—-the little 8 year old riding the waves, the lost and angry college student, the black sheep of the family, the accomplished professional, the community organizer, the radical, the teacher, the wanderer and wonderer, the performer and improviser, the internationalist—and was able to have all of that, at least for that beautiful walk. And I could (at least somewhat) be more comfortable with all the memorable relationships (including, ours) that made me, Me.

OK, yes, on-and-off on this visit, I felt deeply queasy being back in the South—a place I still joke about as the "land where time stood still" (i.e., *circa* 1860!).

But history hasn't stood still. And neither have I.

Thank you, Lois, for your inscrutable advice.

From J.D.

Since writing to "The Developmentalist" (a few times) I am performing differently. With regard to "being a know it all" ("I'm the Most Experienced Person in the Room, so How Do I Learn?" p. 86). now when I enter group environments (classes, workshops, community projects) where I can assume that I'm among newbies and that I'm more skilled and knowledgeable, etc., I'm doing something new. I'm more attentive—"letting in" where I am and who I'm with. I'm less focused on our relative skill level, and more curious about who's in the room and what they bring to our group endeavor. I better appreciate our joint activity as a group learning. And so I'm able to better have the "newness" of who we are together.

A second letter ("I'm Triggered By Trigger Talk," p. 21) I wrote to Lois about being triggered by all the trigger talk (it's everywhere!) was also eye opening. Beyond "being annoyed," I've been more curious about what others are saying—what this talk means to them. I'm paying attention, asking questions.

From Other Readers

From J.B.

Thank you, Lois, for this so-helpful perspective ("I'm Scared Of Dying," p. 79). Me and my family are moving through my father's dying process in real time, and we are creating what meaning, rituals and emotions we want together. This includes having parties and singing to old Elvis songs and reading short stories together. We are sad, yet we're not afraid or tragedy-izing. And trying not to worry as Huey reminds us.

From "Lizzie" Nigeria

Lois, you write:

> Forgiveness isn't a condition for an active, even an intimate, relationship. If it was, nobody would talk to anyone! My thoughts on "letting go of hurt" are similar. You don't have to. What would be helpful and growthful is for you to make the hurt "the size" it deserves to be in your whole life—who you are and are becoming. It's not the totality of YOU. You asked me for performance tips. Sue, I have just one: Lay down your burden.

I follow "The Developmentalist" and have learned so much from the responses to the letters. The response I quote from ("What If I Can't Just Forgive and Forget?" p. 41) from someone who was finding it hard to forgive spoke directly to me. The name "Sue" could comfortably be replaced with "Lizzie."

Before now, I had always felt the need to forgive my dad to effectively build a smooth relationship with him. My dad, a father of 12 children from two wives, was faced with a huge burden upon his shoulders. He needed to provide for all 12 children as well as meet the basic day to day needs of our households. As an adult now, I understand it must have been difficult for him to carry all these burdens; however, my resentment is built on the premise of his choice of priority. While he prioritized most needs of my other siblings, mine were often the disregarded ones. My mother took charge of most of my schooling expenses throughout secondary school and I had to do part time programs to enable me to work and support myself through tertiary education. While this could have been an agreement my parents had in terms of resource management, I needed an explanation for closure as I had often seen my dad as uncaring towards me. I have made up so many excuses to justify his actions but none of these excuses made me feel any better. I had tried to have a conversation with him expressing my pains, but his reasons were not convincing enough. Memories of my struggles still linger especially when compared to the amazing experiences I've heard people share about their fathers.

As an adult, I battle daily with the need to forgive him thinking that forgiveness is needed to build a better relationship between us. However, when I read the above exchange, I realized that sometimes forgiving isn't the only way. We can choose to let go or decide how much space such pain deserves in our lives and that's what I have done. Much to my delight, I have an improved relationship with my dad now as I am able to see beyond that experience and appreciate his efforts in other areas where he was there as a father to my siblings and I. Looking beyond myself, I now see the several sacrifices he made for the family and this is worthy of acknowledgment. With this I have gotten the closure I sought for over 20 years and I see my early exposure to working and schooling as an opportunity that led to self-discovery, career path development, leadership experience and personal growth which helped boost my confidence even as a person with albinism in Nigeria. The pain only had a very small place in my life after all!

Comments from Practitioners

Some of the following practitioners are familiar with my work and make reference to prior experience with the concept/practice of development and/or the varied practices that constitute social therapeutics. Others are not. All are reproduced here with their permission.

Hugh Polk, MD, New York, NY

Good Therapy?

I'm a psychiatrist and practicing social therapist with a longstanding group and family practice. I've worked and trained with Fred Newman and Lois Holzman, the founders of the social therapeutic approach, for most of my professional life since the late 1970s. As a practitioner, I've been an avid fan of "The Developmentalist." I read the letters closely, and play a little game with myself, called "How Would I Respond?" First, I read the letter from the person asking for help. Then, before I read Lois's response, I'll work out my own, and then compare the two. Sometimes, the direction we take has a family resemblance. Other times, I'm surprised and delighted to see that she's gone in a different, interesting *other* direction that I had never even considered. I let that surprise "land" as much as I can and allow myself to savor new ideas and options. I believe I'm becoming more improvisationally versatile as a result.

While Lois is not officially a therapist, in my book "The Developmentalist" is good therapy, because as an advice column it subverts the very activity of giving advice! Lois's observations and questions don't answer. If anything, they raise more questions.

They support people to discover new ways of seeing, being, feeling (with others), and in that process help them deal with difficult/transitional life moments in creative ways—ways they might not have thought of on their own. Likewise, the clinical practice of social therapy helps the group build environments to grow emotionally and otherwise, and in so doing, discover themselves as builders of their lives.

In her correspondences, Lois responds very directly, with brevity and without interpretation. She actively pays attention—"listens"—to the details of what the person has *actually said*. She acknowledges their pain, then homes in on something that could be central to their predicament.

She untangles the "developmental dilemma," with philosophically provocative observations and questions. She'll share her thinking: "I suspect …," or "I wonder …"—but not as a "telling." It's more as an expansive exploration of their subjectivity—a muddling about the linguistic traps and assumptions inherent in their very description of the problem. Then she goes on to suggest new activities, new pathways, new ways to engage with others, to "spring the trap" they're stuck in—to "move around and about it," as Ludwig Wittgenstein famously said.

I've discovered in coming to appreciate Lois's style that I want to grow my capacity to ask my clients philosophically provocative questions that challenge their individualized assumptions about everything. I'm enjoying creatively imitating her and find myself philosophizing with my clients more: "What do you mean by that?" I'll ask. "Where does that idea come from?" "How did you come to understand things that way?"

Clients are sometimes incredulous about my questions. And they can be resistant to suggestions of doing something different with me. They can be skeptical, cynical and scared. Often I'll hear, "Whatever I try, it will *never* work." A patient in one of my groups, for example, insists on seeing himself as a failure and tries to build an airtight case to convince me that he is. I recently asked him,

> Look, you've told me how miserable you are and how glum the world looks and feels from inside your head. So rather than hold on to your need for certainty, would you be open to simply considering how I see you? Instead of arguing with me, could you take an emotional leap, and consider what I'm saying? Could you ask me—someone who knows you well—how come I see you differently? Be curious with me! It might help you let some fresh air into your head!

I think that's what social therapists do on our best days. We openly acknowledge the risk of growth, we acknowledge the "hardness" of development, while inviting new collaborative, social/relational "doings." "The Developmentalist's" query to people we work with comes down to this: "Are you open to building (risky) spaces with me and others where we have a shot at springing the traps, and creating new ways of thinking, seeing, feeling and ultimately, performing our lives?"

From Murray Dabby, LCSW, Atlanta, GA

Let's Build Some Escape Hatches

Lois offers a breath of fresh air to me as a coach and group therapist whose fervent intent is to help my clients address life challenges from a growth perspective, and with less obsession over origins, etiologies, explanations and prescriptions. Let's develop!

I pay attention to Lois's activistic, quizzical and philosophical approach. It has supported me to lead my groups into conversations that can move around and about a "presenting problem" with more questions than answers—with less assumptions, less explanatory baggage—and more out-of-the-box wonderment and heart. I'm thrilled when I can help my groups ditch their fascination with cause and categories, and plunge into creating anew with their emotional pain. "Group, let's build some escape hatches!" I say, echoing Lois.

In my therapy practice, I have shared some of the letters and responses to "The Developmentalist" with clients by way of follow-up to a particular conversation we've had in group. I've forwarded them letters such as, "I'm a Conflicted Romantic," and "I'm Triggered by 'Trigger Talk'," that touch on issues that are so alive in our culture. Sharing with Lois's lovingly challenging observations has led to a furthering of the group's non-psychological investigations! A developmentalist's lens has helped our therapy unfold.

From Jared French, PhD, CPsych, London, ON

What Does Effective Therapy Look Like?

My graduate training was in the field of Counseling Psychology. I felt connected to the Rogerian ideas I was initially exposed to and hoped that relating to people in primarily warm and affirming ways would promote the kinds of changes they desired. I recall an early client that I'd worked with for several sessions calling to end our work together, saying that although I was "a very nice person," they didn't think that therapy was working for them. I thanked the client and let them know that I was more interested in being effective than nice and wondered if they'd be willing to return for one more session to see if we could do something different together. Although I didn't know exactly what that would look like, I knew that I wanted to be more than nice and supportive—I wanted to co-create good therapy with the client.

I experience Lois' column as including many of the same qualities that make for good therapy: 1) Offering empathy and recognition of the other's situation and pain; 2) challenging some assumptions or ways of seeing that may be contributing to feeling stuck; and 3) offering advice that invites new perspectives and ways of going forward. What makes Lois' approach so unique and helpful to me as a therapist is how she does each of the above. She offers empathy without engaging in sentimentality or pitying. She asks questions that are direct and might be hard to hear. And, most significantly in my view, she offers advice that is radically relational. She asks us as her readers to consider saying how we actually feel, and to ask the people in our lives how they feel and what they think. And then, as part of the ongoing process of being relational, to ask if the others in our lives want to creatively build our relationships together in new ways. These are demanding asks, and Lois lets us know that it will take courage and vulnerability to open ourselves up to potentially more hurt, rejection, and pain, but also to the possibility of more connection, understanding, intimacy, and creativity.

Lois' column reminds me that doing therapy in this way is bolstered by:

1. Taking up an historical perspective when tackling current problems and circumstances (see letter: "How Do I Protect My Teens?") where Lois comments on managing kids' social media use being preceded by the introduction of television into North American homes in the 1950s);
2. Exposing and dissolving the seeming dichotomies of "what is", by asking us to consider relating, communicating, questioning, and engaging in curiosity with others in new ways (see letter: "Thanks For Your Advice, But It's Just Not Me"); and,
3. Applying Lois' advice of "Don't do it alone!"—which helps me get away from the perspective that we're all isolated individuals with individual problems that are best suited to be addressed in individual therapy. Instead, Lois invites us to take on our challenges together and build with what we have; that is, the messy, lovely, painful, silly, frantic, fun, and tragic parts of being human (see letter: "I Can't Reach My Students! Help!").

In my full time, day-to-day work as a psychologist, I provide/co-create therapy and at times it's easy to do so in routinized ways. "The Developmentalist" column is a place I'm reminded of the qualities that make for good therapy; that is, creative, demanding, and caring ways of relating with others.

From Joyce Dattner, social therapeutic coach, Jersey City, NJ

Nothing to Fix

I've led weekly emotional development groups and worked with couples, other life partnerships and families for 40-plus years. I was trained by the founder of social therapy, Fred Newman, in his development focused approach to helping people in emotional pain and distress when I was a young community organizer and teacher.

I continue to lean on his intellectual partner, Lois Holzman (and most recently her "The Developmentalist" correspondences) to keep the conversations I create with the people who join our practice at Life Performance Coaching philosophical and relational. I've learned that when left unexamined with playful and philosophically curious questions, therapeutic conversations can go down the rabbit hole of fitting complex emotional responses into predetermined categories. Very painfully, we swiftly become problems to be fixed.

I work to respond to people asking for help in ways that both accept who they are (the pain they're in/the way they talk about the pain they're in) and as capable of going beyond what they (and perhaps others in their lives) believe is possible. I invite them to playfully build conversation with the group that opens new possibilities without attempting to fix anything.

I believe that the ability to care deeply without "fixing" is critically important, though unfortunately not something most therapists and coaches are trained to do. Rather, we are trained (and constrained) to believe our job is to help people solve life's challenges and to relate to those challenges as problems to be sorted and fixed.

In contrast, development doesn't fix. It builds upon an honest acceptance of *what is* as we create *what's possible.*

The heart of the magic/method/politic that I read in these correspondences is a commitment to creating new possibilities with what we've got (with all that our clients bring to our therapeutic work)—"especially when what we've got isn't so hot."

The letter, "I'm an Emotional Mess in a Tragically Messed-Up World," for example, presents just such a developmental dilemma. The letter writer is stuck—wants to be other; wants to stop being so "messed up." Lois responds with: "Embrace your emotional maladjustment and grow from there! You might develop into someone who can 'rile herself up' and rest at the same time!"

I was reminded of this interchange in thinking about one of my groups that I co-lead with Randy Wilson. A client, who I'll call Nina, began talking about how her new marriage wasn't going well. Nina blamed herself for the situation. She explained that she was a "really bad person" who often yells at her husband, is impatient, can be sexually withholding, and isn't always nice. Nina spoke about what it was like growing up with a mother who was often angry and unkind. This only served to strengthen her argument that she was just like her mother and, thus, would always be the problem who needed to be fixed.

Without negating the content of her claim (i.e., "I'm a really bad person"), the group zeroed in on the *activity of her saying to them that she was bad*. Their response was not to dismiss the content of her claim or to assure her that it really wasn't the case she was bad, but to invite her out of her head and back into a building process with them. "Nina, let's look at this together; let's help you lay down the burden of possessing these private judgments. Come (out here!) into our life together" (I'm paraphrasing). Embrace your maladjustment, the group urged her; that's the space from which we can grow emotionally.

And so she did. The group spoke openly—working hard not to blame or shame, not to dismiss or sidestep—but to look, listen, query and invent. Importantly, they explored the assumptions that riddled Nina's defining narrative, and how she'd come to understand herself in these ways and to perform them with others.

I believe that if we leave assumptions about ourselves unexamined, they can be profoundly distortive and stultifying, emotionally and otherwise. The activity of unpacking our assumptions together—socially with a group we have helped to build—creates possibility. It's an acceptance of who-we-are *and* who-we-are-becoming-with-them-and-others. And that's a growth activity.

Nina was deeply touched by participating in creating maybe a first-ever conversation about her emotional limitations where the premise was not that she needed to be fixed. Without a fix, there was now the possibility of emotional growth.

From Maureen Kelly, Brooklyn, NY

I Hear Your Offer and Accept it!

I head Performance of a Lifetime, a global leadership development company that uses performance and improvisation as a catalyst for developing leaders and teams. "The Developmentalist" reinforces what we do and pushes us further.

The "presenting dilemmas" Lois tackles (and her responses) have become a go-to review text in our work. I read the letters regularly to inspire new ways to lead my team of coaches and consultants across the Americas, Asia and Europe and support them to grow as *developmentalists*.

I pay attention to *how* Lois responds—to what she picks up on, to how she listens, to how she lets herself be impacted, to the intentionality with which she lets their offers *land*. I see her capacity to *be with* that person and create with what they give her—their emotionality, premises and phrasing. She often will locate/illuminate the person's dilemma in and of the world, e.g., the cultural expectations of being a mother, or the impact of a broken healthcare system on caring for loved ones.

I liken this mode of listening and questioning as a practice of *radical acceptance*. In the milieu of improvisational theatre it's a first premise, called *accepting an offer*. I coach my team and tell my clients to *accept and let the offers land*, and I put my hand on my heart as I say it to convey that listening is an active and relational activity.

Listening in this way is a rare activity! We are taught as children (and then rewarded as adults) to talk fast and first, to know the most, and to be smart(er). But listening might well be a leader's most powerful (and, too often, most under-utilized) tool. We create environments that support leaders to grow as listeners by performing and practicing how they listen. We do this through improvisational exercises and role-plays that mirror their actual leadership conversations. They discover that listening is a performance and a muscle we need to exercise.

When I read the letters through a slightly different lens, I appreciate how Lois explores the entanglements created by our compulsion to explain, get quick answers, interpret, forecast and diagnose. Lois's training in linguistics—an interest in *how* people do their "languaging"—informs her social therapeutic practice. She writes about it as a practice which draws upon the work of philosopher Ludwig Wittgenstein, who (in his day) tried to cure philosophers of their muddled thinking. Her responses almost always point to how writers have backed themselves into corners with how they speak and reason. This is an area in which I'm actively working to grow in my day-to-day conversations as a leader, consultant, and coach.

From Lenore (Thecla) Farrell, New York, NY

People Persons

I'm from a large family in Trinidad—a country with a population of 1.2 million, and a fun-loving, performatory culture (think: Carnival and dancing through the streets!). I came to the US, to Texas, to study finance. I built a career at an international bank, where in recent years I worked with colleagues from Asia, India, and the Americas. I became recognized for my "people skills"—which when translated, I believe, means I was appreciated for my capacity to lead, organize and support quite diverse stakeholder groups. My Caribbean way of speaking—straightforward, honest and demanding—served us well. I helped organize activities where my teams could be more human, less competitive, more collaborative and creative. Executives paid attention when they saw that work groups who developed these skills could achieve a competitive business edge.

That's only half the story. By day, I performed at the bank. By night and weekends, I brought my love of dance and theatre, and my passion to build a better world, to an off-off-Broadway political theatre. There I performed as a producer, actor, promoter and assistant director. I became saturated in theatre! I learned everything there was to learn about improvisation and building ensembles. My theatre comrades recognized my talents as a "people person" too; and I honed my skills building bridges to other political theatres in the US and Martinique, Germany and France.

Several years ago, I initiated another personal growth spurt. I decided to begin formal training as a group leader and coach. This included spending a year immersing myself in social therapeutics at the East Side Institute (which Lois heads). The methodology was grounded in improvisational performance: i.e., that we grow by performing in other/new plays that we invent with others. We recast ourselves. It was right up my alley. Last year, I hung a shingle at the Life Performance Coaching Center, where I now work with individuals, families and couples.

Which brings me to "The Developmentalist." It's one of the very few materials I read before or after sessions. It's written in ordinary, conversational language (which I like a lot) while presenting seriously unorthodox queries and performance directives. The scope of the letters (from Taiwan, Mexico, India, the US, etc.) helps me get a pulse on what people are grappling with in the Global South and Global North, alike.

Many of my clients bring similar, parallel or maybe almost universal issues into our groups, and I stay close to how our dilemmas and despair are both *in and of this world*. In their pain, I experience how the world is stuck.

Like Lois, I want to be the kind of "director" (in the theatrical sense) who helps clients step into uncharted territory—to wonder together. I want them (and me) to let go of our typically knowing, interpreting, explaining ways of being together. I want my groups to lose themselves in wonderment—to go on a journey that could defy expectations. Who knows what we'll create?

PART THREE
ZOOMING OUT

Chapter 14
The Social Therapeutic Roots of a Developmentalist Practice

In the Prologue to this book, "How It Started," Janet Wootten shares the immediate origins of "The Developmentalist" column and project. This is a reasonable starting point for what has become the book you are now reading. But it is, like all starting points, arbitrary. So much that came before and so much that was happening at the same time as I received and responded to that first letter gave birth to the column and the book. And so, where to begin?

Perhaps the way I began Chapter 1 of my book, *The Overweight Brain: How Our Obsession with Knowing Keeps Us from Getting Smart Enough to Make a Better World*:

> Murray Holzman helped me to become a good knower. He was my father. Fred Newman helped me to become a good grower. He was my mentor and friend. I'm thinking if maybe I tell you something about Murray and me, and Fred and me, you'll get some idea of what I mean by knowing and growing and how I came to distinguish them. (Holzman, 2018a, p. x)

Or with the first line of a chapter I wrote for a handbook of humanistic psychology: "I don't have much use for labels, categories or academic disciplines, except to disrupt them by playing and creating new ones with them" (Holzman, 2016, p. 87).

Or the beginning of a keynote address I delivered at a conference on healing society in Taiwan:

> We have been taught to believe that the past determines the present. Karl Marx challenged this—and posited that it doesn't have to be that way, that the present can determine the past. This has been one of the inspirations of my life. (Holzman, 2015)

Or as the opening to a dialogic chapter written by me and Tomas Pernecky for his book, *Postdisciplinary Knowledge*:

Tomas: I suppose an appropriate way to begin this dialogue on knowledge-as-play is to invite you to play with me. I am interested in exchanging ideas about this topic because I see playfulness and creativity as something that is closely connected with knowledge. Do you want to play?

Lois: What a lovely and challenging offer! Yes, I want to play! Knowing makes our brains heavy. Playing makes it lighter. Playing with knowing—what does that do? We cannot know, but we can play! (Pernecky and Holzman, 2019, no page)

Or with the blind date who brought me to a gathering that introduced me to the world of social change efforts outside of university research departments, and to a community-in-the-making that tolerated my scholarly leanings and learned with me to creatively meld intellectual innovations from the academy with the street smarts of community activists.

The gathering consisted of about three dozen novice activists in their 20s. Several of them left the campus of the City College of New York to join their philosophy professor, Fred Newman, on the streets of New York City. Like millions of others, Newman was radicalized by events of the 1960s. Believing that profound social change would not come from the university campus, Newman stopped teaching philosophy and left academia. He and these students set up community organizing collectives in working-class neighborhoods of New York City. From these beginnings in the 1960s has grown what has come to be known as a *development community* of tens of thousands, in the US and globally (Holzman, 2014a, 2016, 2020a).

Newman had a solid training in both western and eastern philosophy, most particularly in the philosophy of science and language and in the British and American analytic and pragmatism traditions. He brought this to everything he built and to his exploration of revolutionary movements, both political and intellectual. This attracted me to the fledgling movement Newman was building for, while I had no formal training in philosophy, my own discontent with the experimental methodology, individualistic bias, and pretense of political neutrality that permeated social science and educational research practices had, I soon discovered, a philosophical basis.

In 1976, when I first met these activists, I had just completed my PhD in developmental psychology and psycholinguistics at Columbia University and joined the Laboratory for Comparative Human Cognition, a research lab at Rockefeller University headed by American cultural psychologist Michael Cole.

There we began to tie what we saw to be the scientific invalidity of the conceptions and methods of experimental cognitive psychology to the racial and class biases of educational practices in US schools. We carried out a series of studies with school-age children, both in and outside of schools, developing methods of what has come to be known as qualitative research (Cole, Hood, and McDermott, 1994; Hood and McDermott, 1980).

It was there that my serious interest in the work of Lev Vygotsky and his social-cultural understanding of human development began. With a few colleagues, Michale Cole was just completing the translation of some of Vygotsky's writings, published as *Mind in Society*, the book that popularized Vygotsky's thought in the English-speaking world (Vygotsky, 1978). In addition to inspiring our studies at the lab, Vygotsky's relevance to broader social transformation seemed promising to me, and I shared it with Newman and the group of activists. Vygotsky's dialectical methodology and his understanding of the *cultural and relational processes* of human development, learning, language, and play continue, over the decades, to shape the many projects and activities of the development community. They have, in turn, shaped me as a developmentalist.

When I refer to Vygotsky's dialectical methodology, I mean, first and foremost, that he saw his task as one of developing a psychology that didn't destroy the integrity of the complexity of humans as social beings who create culture and have histories, both a species history and our individual histories. Vygotsky was an important figure in the debates in the early 20th century over the direction psychology would take. Well on its way to becoming an empirical and experimental science, its methods and units of analysis were hotly debated at the time. A critical question was whether following an experimental path would mean that human consciousness would be excluded from psychological investigation.

Vygotsky was not willing to give up the study of consciousness with a psychology that reduced mental events to non-mental ones, or settle for two kinds of psychology—a subjective one for mental events and an objective one for non-mental events. These options, he argued, rested on an erroneous belief in an objectivist epistemology, which, in effect, denies science as a human (meaning-making) activity and mistakenly treats human beings as natural phenomena. For Vygotsky, psychology as a human science could not develop so long as it was based in objective-subjective dualism. The method of natural science might work for studying natural phenomena but not for the study of human beings. A psychology with a natural science method contains "an insoluble methodological contradiction. It is a natural science about unnatural things" and produces "a system of knowledge which is contrary to them" (Vygotsky, 2004, p. 298). Instead, what was needed to study human beings was a non-dualistic method, a precondition of which was a non-dualistic *conception of method*. As he put it,

> The search for method becomes one of the most important problems of the entire enterprise of understanding the uniquely human forms of psychological activity. In this case, the method is simultaneously prerequisite and product, the tool and the result of the study. (Vygotsky, 1978, p. 65)

This represents a radical break with the accepted scientific paradigm in which method is a tool that is applied and yields results. In that case, the relation between tool and result is linear, instrumental, and dualistic. It is a *tool for result methodology* (Newman and Holzman, 1993/2013). What Vygotsky is proposing is a different conception of method—not a tool to be applied but an activity (a "search") that generates both tool and result at the same time and as a continuous process. Tool and result are not dualistically separated, neither are they the same or one thing. They are elements of a dialectical unity/totality/whole. Vygotsky is advocating that method be practiced, not applied. He is introducing something new—a *tool-and-result methodology* (Newman and Holzman, 1993/2013).

The distinction between tool and result and tool for result is relevant to how people of any culture see and relate to themselves and the people and stuff of the world. In the west, we have been socialized to see through the lens of the problem–solution paradigm. Problems are the "stuff" of life in the western(ized) world, and with problems come solutions, even if they are not always realized. People see and understand themselves and others in terms of and in the language of problems. We are taught to see problems and to search for solutions. Doing "good" science (or good diplomacy, education, government, therapy, and so on) has come to mean correctly identifying the problems and coming up with solutions to them. Despite the failure of this mode of seeing and thinking in the human development realm (for example, raising children, living peacefully, or eliminating poverty), the problem–solution paradigm dominates, severely constraining people's capacity to envision possibilities of transforming the world.

The distinction between tool and result and tool for result also helps us see more clearly how our culture adapts us to see and experience things and products as isolated particulars at different points in time. This "thingification" blinds us to process. And that produces alienation which, in its classic Marxist sense, is relating to the products of production severed from their producers and from the process of their production—that is, as commodities. This way of relating is not limited to cars, loaves of bread, and computers. It is the normal way of seeing and relating to everything in contemporary western culture. People relate to their lives, their relationships, their feelings, their knowledge, and so on, as things, torn away from the process of their creation and from their creators. This alienation is a key factor in people's relational lives and emotional angst. It is an impediment to the developmental process of continuous qualitative transformation. It leaves us susceptible to relying on identities ("This is the kind of person I am—I can't change") and stages ("Teenagers are like that") and diagnostic labels ("He's an alcoholic") as explanatory. End of story. Many of my responses to the letters in Chapters 3–11 invite exploration of these kinds of constraining assumptions.

Can we become less commodified and less alienated? Can we engage in activity that allows us not only to glimpse process but to experience ourselves as the producers of that process *and* of the products it yields? Can we create stages for development *and* development? Can we, in other words, create tools and results? We certainly can.

Very early on in the activist work of creating a development community, we recognized that this alienation was the primary subjective factor keeping people from actively working together to create the kinds of lives (and, indeed, the kind of world) they wanted. We invited people to join us in creating new kinds of schools, theatres and cultural activities, youth programs, health groups, anti-poverty programs, and more. Each of these projects was mindful of the emotional challenges of diverse people working together, of focusing equally on process and products, and of the risks involved in going against the grain, and they addressed these challenges to some degree. But one project, in particular, took on emotionality (or the mass psychology of alienation) as its focus. That project was social therapy, a non-diagnostic, cultural approach to engaging emotional distress and pain. It was conceived of, practiced, and developed at the East Side Institute (eastsideinstitute.org), one of the earliest organizations Newman and I founded.

Challenging Psychology's Assumptions

Social therapy originated in the 1970s along with many other social-cultural change movements of the time that tied the "personal" to the political. Like the radical therapies (e.g., Black, gay, and feminist) springing up at the time, social therapy engaged the hegemonic cultural biases of authoritarianism, sexism, racism, classism, and homophobia as manifest in mainstream psychotherapy. Social therapy also engaged the conceptual biases of the dominant culture. It drew attention to the philosophical underpinnings of the institutions and practices of psychology and psychotherapy and rejected explanation, interpretation, the notion of an inner self that therapists and clients need to delve into, and other dualistic and problematic foundations of traditional psychology—a characteristic of dozens of therapeutic approaches that now fall under the rubric of postmodern psychologies (e.g., Gergen, 2000, 2001; Holzman and Morss, 2000; Kvale, 1992).

Perhaps the most pervasive assumption that guides the dominant understanding and practices of psychology and psychotherapy is the problem–solution paradigm, discussed above. We live in a culture that problematizes emotional life. Going to a therapist means that something is wrong, and the therapist's first task is to identify the "presenting problem." For the mainstream psychotherapist, the work is finding the solution to the problem, first by naming it and then by going through (sometimes with the client, sometimes not) a process of discovering the cause or source of the problem or by prescribing medication, or by some combination of the two. Institutionalized psychotherapy is so organized around problems that if you do not have one that is identifiable according to the *Diagnostic and Statistical Manual of Mental Disorders* (*DSM*), you can be denied treatment (e.g., EDNOS—"eating disorder not otherwise specified," Henig, 2004).

The *DSM-5*, the 2013 revision of the manual published by the American Psychiatric Association, was a source of great controversy and much publicity from 2011 through its publication in May 2013. While much of the outcry had to do with the pseudo-scientific way the manual was generated, an equal amount came from parents and service providers concerned that changes in diagnostic categories would reduce or even eliminate needed services. Among the most controversial was the elimination of Asperger's syndrome as a distinct disorder and its incorporation into autism spectrum disorder—the fear being that there would no longer be a category of mental illness to draw on for reimbursement (Singh, 2011).

More broadly, there has been decades-long criticism of diagnosis as a requirement for psychotherapy, including pleas to abandon the medical model and view psychotherapy as an art and not a science (*Journal of Humanistic Psychology*, 2017–2019). However, there is less critical discussion of the problem–solution paradigm that underlies it. Pointing out that the person is not the problem but "has" a problem, for example, does not deny the problem–solution paradigm.

The methodology with which to tackle a world filled with problems is an instrumental one. The tool-for-result methodology is the epistemological counterpart to the ontology of problems and solutions. It is essentially a problem-solving approach.

In contrast, the tool-and-result methodology rejects this way of viewing and living in the world in favor of a more unified, emergent, and continuous-process approach. The goal of psychotherapy of the tool-and-result variety, including social therapy, is to support people to create, not to problem solve. Psychotherapies of this type are collaborative, with therapists and clients together creating the therapy. They are exercises in meaning making. Above all, they are relational, not only in focusing on the co-creative relationship of therapists and clients but also in seeing and relating to emotion as relational.

John Shotter has been a leading voice in exploring the relational basis of human subjectivity and the "otherness" in human relations and bringing into his work Bakhtin, Voloshinov, Vygotsky, and Wittgenstein (Shotter, 1991, 1993a, 1993b). McNamee and Gergen's collection of essays, *Therapy as Social Construction*, introduced relational, meaning-making, and non-objectivist counseling and therapy practices (1992). Ten years later, Lock and Strong's edited volume *Discursive Perspectives in Therapeutic Practice* shared advances made in relational, meaning-making, and non-objective counseling and therapy practices (Lock and Strong, 2012). In social therapeutic practices, the relational work, in tool-and-result fashion, involves creating new emotionality inseparable from new ways of relating to emotionality.

How is emotionality related to in general? To put it bluntly, our culture has not been kind to emotion. It has been ignored, demeaned, and cast aside as inferior to cognition, the enemy of rationality, characteristically female (and, thereby, unworthy of attention) for centuries. While feminist psychologists and philosophers have made significant contributions in exposing the male biases of accepted conceptions of being human since the 1960s, the overall cultural environment of psychology, both theoretically and institutionally, remains paradigmatically male and cognitively overdetermined. Psychotherapy, the area of psychology most identified with emotion, is generally thought of as soft science, or not science at all. This assessment is applauded by those who relate to psychotherapy as an art or cultural activity and lamented by those who work to advance its scientific credentials.

The last two decades have seen the profession bowing to pressure or taking up the mantle (depending on one's point of view) to become more "scientific" (objective, measurable, "evidence-based," etc.), even as female psychotherapists outnumber their male counterparts, a trend also noted for psychology as a whole (*American Psychologist*, 2006, and www. apa.org/gradpsych/2011/01/cover-men.aspx). A welcome innovation occurring in the profession is the shift to relationality (which makes use of the feminist conception of connection). But, in the overall conservative environment in which this shift is taking place, relationality is not only marginalized but highly vulnerable to being cast in cognitive terms.

Mainstream psychology's objects of study are the individual and behavior. In keeping with this, emotion is located within the individual, and emotional development is understood in terms of stages (e.g., Erikson's eight crises of psychosocial development). While there has been an increase in interest in emotional development since the turn of the century, emotion is typically related to cognitively, behavioristically, and normatively. For example, psychologists identify the stages at which children should become able to "regulate" their emotions and learn the social-cultural rules of emotional expression. Further, recent discoveries in neuroscience pertaining to emotion have been used by many psychologists to support a regulatory objective.

The dominant psychotherapeutic approaches, such as cognitive and behavioral therapies, see emotions as caused by certain problematic cognitions. So dominant is cognition that the field of psychotherapy did not pay much attention to emotions until fairly recently when it began to market emotions as an important topic in psychotherapy, perhaps to remedy the absence of emotion in training programs and the litera- ture. The past two decades have seen a proliferation of books, articles, and conferences that frame clients' emotional lives as a new frontier in psychotherapy and offer therapists opportunities to learn how to make use of emotions in their therapeutic encounters. For example, the 2011 American Academy of Psychotherapists conference was themed, "The Role of Emotion in Psychotherapy," with the following rationale:

> because of recent trends in academic psychology and research-based training programs, emotional processes and the need for expressive/experiential affective interventions have been under-valued or eschewed as important clinical skills. Hence the need to reinforce the value of the role of emotions in psychotherapy. (2011, www.aapweb.com/files/SouthernRegion_Brochure_4-11.pdf)

Another example is the popular online resource for therapists, the Psychotherapy Networker, which promoted its 2012 series, "The Power of Emotions," as a way for practitioners to

> Gain the understanding, insight, and know-how to engage authentically with clients as emotions emerge [because] working with emotions can be tough for both clients and therapists. This series is designed both to deepen your understanding of emo- tions and to strengthen your ability to work with them effectively. (Psychotherapy Networker, 2012, www.psychotherapynetworker. org/cecourses/networker-plugged-in/emotion-web-series)

Continuing this focus on emotions, the *Networker* currently offers the online course "The Healing Power of Emotions" as a way to "enhance your practice" (https://catalog.psychotherapynetworker.org/sales/pn_c_ 001097_healingpowerofemotion_organic-15951 online course).

Emotion-focused therapy has become its own recognized approach to psychotherapy. "*Emotion-focused therapy* (EFT) can be defined as the practice of therapy informed by an understanding of the role of emotion in psychotherapeutic change" (www.apa.org/pubs/books/ Emotion-Focused-Therapy-Ch-1-Sample.pdf 9.20.24, http://dx.doi. org/10.1037/15971-001).

At least in part, the surge of interest in emotion is coming from discoveries in neuroscience—which, even from reading only the popular press, seem to be made each day (and which are fascinating). But what are others doing with these discoveries? Quoting the Psychotherapy Networker again,

> Neuroscientists have recently established that emotion is the prime organizing force shaping how we cope with challenges ... emotion is anything but primitive and unpredictable. It's a complex, exquisitely efficient information-processing system, designed to organize behavior rapidly in the interests of survival. (www.psychotherapynetworker.org/magazine/recentissues/2012-mayjune/item/1702-the-power-of-emotion-in-therapy)

To me, this sounds like a typical description of cognition. It seems that, in order to bring emotionality to the attention of therapists, it has to be framed in cognitive terms, which, apparently, legitimizes it.

In situating social therapy in relation to typical and dominant understandings of emotions and the practices based on these understandings, I hope to have given you a greater appreciation for the unconventionality of a developmentalist's approach. Relating to people as creators of emotions, and to emotions as social-cultural relational activities changes the responsibility of both practitioners and clients. Don't regulate, don't repress, don't possess, don't explain. Instead, share, make offers, play with, perform anew. Grow your emotional repertoire.

No doubt you have noticed that my responses to letters I receive often make the suggestion to share what's going on emotionally, to make what might seem to be a risky offer in a conversation, to play with one's seeming dilemma, and/or to try a new performance (of worry, sadness, anger, and so on) with others. And no doubt you would like some clarification or explication of what I mean. Once again, I turn to Vygotsky for some help.

In his search to create method consistent with a social-cultural-historical approach in psychology, Vygotsky focused much of his research and scholarship on children. In Chapter 1, I provided a brief summary of his insights on children's learning and development and the central role of play in those processes. Here, I will expand upon the role of play, its link to performing, and their role in social and emotional growth at all ages.

Recall Vygotsky's "head taller" metaphor: "In play a child always behaves beyond his average age, above his daily behavior; in play it is as though he were a head taller than himself" (Vygotsky, 1978, p. 102). In their free and pretend play, children create imaginary situations, often incorporating people, things, and events from their experience in fantastical ways (becoming a lion tamer for their stuffed animals after a trip to the zoo, for example). They free themselves from the constraints of real life and, to the extent that there are rules for what can happen, it is the children themselves who make them up while they are playing.

For example, when young children take a pencil and make horse-like movements with it, they are simultaneously creating this imaginary situation and the "rules" of the play (keep jumping, make whinnying sounds, don't write on the paper). When children are playing Mommy and baby, the new meaning that the imaginary situation creates also creates the "rules" of the play (for example, the ways that Mommy and baby relate to each other "in character"). In these examples, everything—the children who are playing, the pencil, the horse, Mommy and baby—are what/who they are and, at the same time, other than what/who they are. That is what "a head taller" means to me. Without knowing they are doing it, young children are playing at being someone else and doing things they have never done. We could say they are simultaneously creating the scene and improvisationally performing it. Indeed, performance is an apt substitute for the word play. It might even enhance our understanding, for performance evokes the magic of the theatre—its deliberate invitation to imagine and be captivated by people on stage being other than who they are, to play along with the players. Just as children go "beyond" their normal behavior as if "a head taller" in play, so too do performers on stage.

Performance in early childhood is not in the performers' awareness. Adults and little children together create the "stage" and perform on it without any awareness that they're performing. Nevertheless, the countless "conversations" like this one—"Mama, baba, bababababa," "Yes, sweetie, that's a little baby doll"—*both create and are* the scenes in an ongoing performance of "The Life of the Developing Baby." In contrast, performers on the theatrical stage are aware that they're performing, and so is the audience. This kind of deliberate performance highlights, experientially, the being–becoming dialectical "space" in which we live and in which development is always potential.

Studying these performances in early childhood and on theatrical stages and exploring what the casts of characters are doing as they build the different stages and scenes (as my colleagues and I have done) reveal how the capacity to create new performances of ourselves as individuals and groupings (classroom, family, work team, community, etc.) is essential to learning and development at any age. Through the lens of performance, we can see development as the activity of building stages and scenes of a play rather than scaffolds and ladders (Holzman, 1997a). Speaking the language of theatrical performance—stages, scenes, characters, and so on—allows us to see performance as a characteristic and an activity that human beings engage in in the most mundane of situations.

Performance is a form of Vygotskian play through which human beings collectively perform their development. For most adults, the non-knowing, imaginative activity of play and the support for "performing a head taller" dissipate beyond childhood. Work, learning, and tasks take over. In order for people to continue to develop and learn developmentally, they need to relearn how to play as children do, but in ways that are appropriate to being adults. They need support to perform a head taller. Social therapy groups are one such support.

Since babies and actors on the stage are supported to be who they are and other than who they are, you may be wondering if it is possible for the rest of us. Newman and I did, and we set out to find out. What would we see if we looked at what people are doing in social therapy groups through a performance lens? What would happen if we related to students and teachers as creators of performances of learning? Could we create environments in which doctors and patients and police officers and teens could stop acting their identity roles, if only briefly, and perform together *as human beings*? (My book *Vygotsky at Work and Play* details what happened when we actualized these situations (Holzman, 2009, 2016). I invite you to take a few minutes and add your own wonderings to mine.

Zones of Emotional Development

The development that people create through actualizing the being–becoming dialectic through play and performance would not occur were it not a social, relational activity. The actors may be reciting a playwright's words, but it is the cast constituted as an ensemble that is performing the play. Babies cannot build the stage for their babbling to transform into meaningful words of a language by themselves. They and their caregivers are carrying out "a collective way of *playing* together" (adding to

Vygotsky's "a collective way of working together" (see below), which is how he described the *zone of proximal development* (ZPD).

The ZPD appears at different times and in multiple translations of Vygotsky's writings, yielding varying understandings of the ZPD discussed by those in education and the social sciences who use his work. And, while the descriptions of the ZPD differ, it is always seen as a social phenomenon. The characterization of the ZPD most relevant to a developmentalist's practice is the one that emphasizes its social collectivity. For example, in "The Collective as a Factor in the Development of the Abnormal Child," Vygotsky characterized the social level of development as "a function of collective behavior, as a form of cooperation or cooperative activity" (Vygotsky, 2004, p. 202).

Linking this with Vygotsky's tool-and-result method, the ZPD becomes a collective activity whereby the creating of the "zone" simultaneously produces the learning and development of the collective. In this sense, the ZPD is a process rather than a thing, and an activity rather than a place, space, or distance. The ZPD highlights the being–becoming dialectic of human life. Creating the ZPD involves relating to people as capable of doing what they do not yet know how to do and what is, therefore, beyond them—what Vygotsky described as "the child's potential to move from what he is able to do to what he is not" (Vygotsky, 1987, p. 212). As applied to social therapy groups, people collectively work together and create the "zone of emotional development" that *is* their new emotionality. As in the ZPD of childhood described by Vygotsky, people at different levels of experience and skill employ a creative methodology of producing environments in which and how they organize and reorganize their relationships to themselves, to each other, and to the tools (both material and psychological) and objects of their world. They construct "zones" that allow them *to become*.

Young children are not yet socialized to the cultural norm that one *must know*. They have not yet evolved the "epistemic posture" (Holzman, 2009). In their relational activity, they are engaging with family members and others in activities they do not yet know how to do, they learn, and they become able to do these things because others support them to actively take risks. We can look at group therapy—in particular social therapy, because of the heterogeneity of its groups—in a similar way. People do not know how to do "therapy talk" when they walk into the therapist's office. They do not know how to create a cooperative way of talking together. The therapist supports them to take risks and do what they don't know how to do. Group therapy maximizes the potential growth because clients must build active relationships with others at varying levels of skill, knowledge, expertise, ability, and personality—that is, they create a ZPD for their emotional growth. The source of that growth is their co-created activity.

Most social therapists prefer groups to individual therapy because groups have more potential to challenge particularism and individualism. The group is the therapeutic unit. This is different from most group therapies, where the group is not itself the therapeutic unit but is a context for the therapist to help individuals with their issues. Clients who come together to form a social therapy group are given the task to create their group as an environment in which they can get help. This group activity is a collective, practical challenge to the assumption that the way people get therapeutic help is to relate to themselves and be related to by others as individuals, complete with problems and with inner selves.

Social therapy groups conducted in centers for social therapy in the US comprise 10–25 people, a mix of women and men of varying ages, ethnicities, sexual orientations, class backgrounds and economic status, professions, and "presenting problems." The groups are consciously heterogeneous for two reasons: (1) To challenge people's notion of a fixed identity (e.g., based on gender, ethnicity, diagnostic label, or "That's the kind of person I am"); and (2) the more diverse the elements, the more material there is to create with. Groups are typically ongoing and meet weekly for 90 minutes. Some group members remain for years, others for months; people leave, and new members join. In this way, the elements of the emotional ZPD are continuously changing. Some social therapists also do teen groups, children's groups, family groups, and partners' groups, keeping them as diverse as possible within these groupings. In other countries, social therapy can look very different from this, as it is practiced in ways that are culturally coherent.

People come to social therapy, as they do to any therapy or any group setting, individuated. They say things like, "My daughter and I were screaming at each other last night. I was so angry at her and now I feel awful"; "I couldn't get out of bed this week"; "I don't know how to talk to my father since he got so sick"; "I feel really crazy, like I'm not here, and it scares me." They look to the therapist for some advice, solution, interpretation, or explanation. They want to feel better and have more control over their lives.

The members of social therapy groups come together and participate in creating their group. The social therapist works with the group
to organize itself as a *zone of emotional development*. Members of the
group raise whatever they want and however they want, which is typically
how they're feeling, an emotional problem, a relationship going bad,
or something upsetting that happened to them. This is the material the
group has to work with. The members, each at different levels of emotional development, are encouraged, invited, supported, and challenged
to create *the group's* level of emotional development. The group has to
figure out how to talk about what they want to talk about.

In western cultures, people relate to feelings as individuated and private, which contributes to people feeling isolated and alone with the
"possession" of their feelings. At some point, the group will recognize
this as an offer and begin creating a relational understanding and language of emotionality. The group members babble, play with language,
listen, build upon each other improvisationally, and make meaning
together. Speaking as truth telling, reality representing, inner thought
and feeling revealing—these deeply held (if, typically, not in conscious
awareness) beliefs about the functions of language are challenged as people falteringly attempt to converse in new ways, to create something new
out of their initial individuated, problem-oriented presentations of self.

The social therapist co-creates with the group this activity of discovering a method of relating to emotional talk relationally rather than indi-
vidualistically, and as activistic rather than as representational. In this
process, people can come to appreciate what—and that—they can create.
They simultaneously come to realize the limitations of trying to learn,
grow, and create individually. If, and as, the group gradually comes to
understand this, different members at different moments realize that
*growth comes from participating in the process of building the groups in
which one functions*. Traditional therapy's focus on the individuated self
who discovers deeper insights into his or her consciousness is transformed into the collective engaged in the continuous activity of creating
a new social unit, the zone of emotional development. The therapeutic
question transforms from "How is each individual doing?" to "How well
is the group performing its activity?"

Such a shift in focus from the individual to the group reorganizes
what is traditionally related to as a dualistic and antagonistic relationship between individual and group into a dialectical one. Mainstream
psychology has tended to negate the group or reduce the group to the

individual. This need not be the case. Recognizing the groupness of human life does not inevitably negate individuals. The group is engaged in producing something collectively, and, as with many life activities, individual members contribute in different ways and to differing degrees. More often than not, group members gain newfound appreciation for the unique person each of them is.

As a developmentalist, I see this activity of creating zones of emotional development as a relearning of how to learn developmentally—that is, learning collectively, playfully, and not cognitively overdetermined. Like what happens when children become languagers, adult social therapy clients are encouraged to do what is beyond them to create new ways of speaking and listening to each other and new ways to understand and relate to talk, to emotions, and to emotional talk. By their language play, they are creating new performances of themselves as a way out of the rigidified roles, patterns, and identities that cause so much emotional pain. They don't necessarily get rid of the emotions they have, but they do create new emotions that are now in their repertoire. By expanding that repertoire, their existing emotions are relocated to "make room" for the new ones. That's what developing emotionally means to me.

It's important to note that this kind of emotional development need not be confined to a therapy office. It can happen anywhere people are supported to create environments in which the possibility for growth is manifest.

Growing Developmentalists

Now that I have situated a developmentalist's practice in social therapy, and situated social therapy within challenges to traditional psychology's and psychotherapy's assumptions and the practices based on them, it is time to shift our gaze further outward. As mentioned at the beginning of Chapter 14, what began 50 years ago with a small group of activists in New York City "searching for method" to make a better world has become a global development community. It is an ever-emergent community that creates development and supports the development it creates. This community took social therapy out of the therapy office, reshaping it many times over in dozens of nations and cultures and making it relevant to adults, teens, children, families, and institutions of all sorts. The community named it social therapeutics to capture the shift from the practice of therapy to the practice of a broad-based approach to human development and learning and community building.

How this happened was not planned or even intentional. As people—including educators, social workers, community organizers, doctors, and nurses—experienced or learned of social therapy, as teachers and youth workers read about how we were making use of Vygotsky's work, as play and performance practitioners and researchers heard our articulation of the ways that performance helps people and communities grow, they increasingly asked to learn our approach.

In the early 2000s, we launched two experimental activities as community-building responses to this interest: Performing the World (www.performingtheworld.org) and the International Class (https:// eastsideinstitute.org/study/international-class/).

As we became aware of the increasing number of people world-wide who were experimenting with the creative arts and performance approaches to psychological and social issues, we decided to host a con-ference on performance and, in early 2001, put out a call for proposals. We and our partners in this, the Taos Institute, called it Performing the World (PTW) and, in October of that year, 120 people from 14 countries showed up. The institute hosted nine more in-person PTWs (in part-nership with the All Stars Project), each with 300–500 participants (Friedman, 2021), and, since 2020, has hosted four virtual PTWs, each attended by hundreds of people. Performing the World is currently a global community of hundreds, from dozens of countries, who explore the power of performance and play to create a better world. It is a leader of the building of an emerging movement that brings development through play, performance, and the arts to citizens to creatively engage social problems and educate, heal, and activate others, to bring new social-cultural-psychological and political possibilities into existence.

The international interest in social therapeutics, as well as that first PTW in 2001, showed us that there was a critical mass that wanted to train with us. We responded, and, two years later in 2003, the institute launched the International Class, a ten-month course of study in social therapeutics and performance activism. The International Class com-bined virtual study and conversation with three immersive residencies in New York City until the COVID-19 pandemic, when it went all virtual. It has remained virtual until the present day.

The 2024–25 cohort of 13 people is the 21st International Class. As of 2025, there are 200 graduates from 44 countries. They come from psychology, psychotherapy, education, social work, theatre, dance, music, creative arts therapies, counseling, medicine, humanitarian aid, and community organizing. Some have established positions at NGOs or in universities. Others are grassroots community workers. Many were already exploring the use of play, improvisation, performance, theatre, or other creative arts and storytelling in their work. Some are pioneers and innovators. Others are radicals in spirit and impassioned about bringing about profound social change All are committed to empowering individuals and communities, whether they are involved with refugees, marginalized communities, homeless and poor youth, prisoners, or educational, therapeutic, or rehabilitation institutions.

With the International Class, social therapeutics became global and has grown dozens of developmentalists in educational, counseling, medical, youth work, psychiatric, cross-cultural, and social justice institutions and organizations. You can meet some of them and learn about their projects at eastsideinstitute.org.

CHAPTER 15
STILL WONDERING? LEARN MORE.

I hope that this book has got you thinking and given you many ideas of how you and others might transform your lives in everyday ways. I also hope that these pages sparked your curiosity and generated dozens of wonderings. This chapter is an invitation to go further. It includes brief descriptions of print, audio, and video resources by myself, my colleagues, and many others on key topics central to the history, context, and practice of a developmentalist (citations appear in the References.) Far from comprehensive, it is a deeply personal list. Happy exploring!

The Overweight Brain: A Companion to A Developmentalist's Guide to Better Mental Health

I wrote *The Overweight Brain: How Our Obsession with Knowing Keeps Us from Getting Smart Enough to Make a Better World* a few years ago. In it I share how I understand what it means to know in our current culture and how our obsession with knowing is so very destructive to mind, body, and spirit. Chapters on schools, psychology, and education illustrate how the "knowing paradigm" plays out to disastrous effect. Other chapters put forth the features of non-knowing growing, or developing. Since I wrote *The Overweight Brain* first, I initially thought of it as a precursor to *A Developmentalist's Guide to Better Mental Health*, but I realize now it's equally a sequel. (That's why I call it a companion.) I would love for you to read it.

Social Therapy and Social Therapeutics

In a way, every time my colleagues and I write or speak, it's about some aspect of social therapy or social therapeutics. We've done it in so many different styles and connected to so many different topics that it could take an entire book to summarize that body of work. Instead, I've chosen three seminal works that illuminate a developmentalist's practice which you might want to begin with.

Psychological Investigations: A Clinician's Guide to Social Therapy

For many years, Fred Newman led supervisory sessions and colloquia for social therapists and therapists in training. Each was a lively and rich discussion of the hows and how-tos of this group-oriented practice of emotional development. I studied my own notes and the transcripts of each session and, with colleague Rafael Mendez, put them together thematically and added introductions by Mendez and me. The result, *Psychological Investigations* (2003), contains over 70 dialogues on the social therapeutic group process; the client–patient relationship; social therapy's applications in health care, alternative medicine, education, and youth work; and issues relevant to various psychotherapeutic approaches. It was a labor of love!

Social Therapeutic Coaching: A Practical Guide to Group and Couples Work

Being non-diagnostic and focusing on ongoing development, social therapeutics can sometimes sound just like coaching. Two social therapeutic practitioners, Carrie Sackett and Murray Dabby—colleagues of mine—think so too. Their 2023 book sheds new light on social therapeutics as a developmental practice by weaving it together with the history and practice of coaching. The book is filled with case studies drawn from the authors' decades of practice. The result is a very practical guide (in a way, a how-to) for anyone working with groups and/or couples. If concrete suggestions and illustrations are what you want, I invite you to read this book.

"Constructing Social Therapeutics"

If the brief discussion of the transition from social therapy conducted in an office to social therapeutics practiced anywhere left you with some wonderings, I invite you to read "Constructing Social Therapeutics"

(Holzman, 2020a). It appears in the *Sage Handbook of Social Constructionist Practice* (mentioned below; McNamee et al., 2020).

Lev Vygotsky

I hope that I have piqued your interest in Lev Vygotsky, since he still inspires me to this day. Something in the wealth of materials described below might inspire you.

Works by Vygotsky

(Most of these works are available for free download at the Marxist Internet Archive https://www.marxists.org)

Mind in Society

This is the easiest of Vygotsky's writings to read. It is a collection of essays from his voluminous body of work. In it, you'll find not only his understandings of learning and development, thinking and speaking and writing, and play in early childhood, but also how he reached them. It was where I got my first taste of Vygotsky and it left me wanting more.

The Vygotsky Reader

Vygotskian scholar Rene Van der Veer brought together a collection of Vygotsky's writings on education, psychology, paedology (child development), psychiatry, and "defectology" (translation of the Russian word for abnormalities such as deafness) (Van dee Veer and Valsiner, 1994). This is where I first read the brilliant article "The Problem of the Environment" (Vygotsky, 1994), which I recommend highly.

The Collected Works of L.S. Vygotsky

Most of these six volumes are challenging but completely worthwhile if you want to see Vygotsky's method in action. One of the biggest challenges is that you'll be reading his descriptions of and challenges to dozens of psychologists of his day that you've never heard of, as he step by step refutes their concepts and findings. However, you will get an inside view of the struggles there were in formulating what psychology might be in its early days.

Works about Vygotsky

If you are interested in how Vygotsky's work has influenced and contributed to contemporary scholarship, research, and practice, especially in education and psychology, here are a film and a book to fill in
the picture: "Lev Vygotsky: One Man's Legacy through His Life and
Theory" (Lowe, 2008; www.youtube.com/watch?v=tqjmQ6ts4SA) and
Revisiting Vygotsky for social change: Bringing together theory and practice
(Neto, Liberali, and Dafermos, 2020).

Everyone I know who has seen this full-length film made in 2008 is
impressed with its breadth. It tells the compelling story of Vygotsky's
times and features a global group of contemporary Vygotskians speaking
of their Vygotstkian-inspired work.

Revisiting Vygotsky for Social Change: Bringing Together Theory and Practice

In 2020, a group of Brazilian scholars published this volume of chapters by
an international group of authors (Neto, Liberali, and Dafermos, 2020).
Their contributions expand Vygotsky's legacy to global contemporary
needs, including social dynamics and human development, ethical-polit-
ical situations of power, the relationship of the human being with society,
and awareness of the social environment. I was proud to be invited to
contribute. My chapter in this book, "Vygotsky on the Margins," presents Vygotsky as a developmentalist and shares the practices of educators
and mental health workers from different parts of the world who were
introduced to Vygotsky through the work of the institute rather than a
university (Holzman, 2020b).

Works about Vygotsky by Yours Truly

If you want to immerse yourself in the history and rationale for me, the
institute, and social therapeutics relating to Vygotsky as a developmentalist, you might try these two books.

Lev Vygotsky: Revolutionary Scientist

In the early 1990s, colleagues who were editing a series on critical psychology for the academic publisher Routledge asked Fred Newman

and me to write a book on Vygotsky for the series. We jumped at the chance to bring threads of our practice and our philosophy together and bring them both to a deeper study of Vygotsky's work. *Lev Vygotsky: Revolutionary Scientist*, published in 1993, was the "product"—our first attempt to articulate what was important to us about his life and work, to present "our Vygotsky." Our unique (at the time) argument that he was primarily a Marxist methodologist was illustrated through a deep dive into his ideas on the dialectical relationship between learning and development, the zone of proximal development as social activity, and the unity of thinking and speaking, among other things. A classic edition of the book was published in 2013 with a new introduction summarizing much that had transpired in the two intervening decades.

Vygotsky at Work and Play

In the early 2000s, both the interest in Vygotsky and interest in social therapeutics were fast increasing worldwide. I had learned so much from the dozens of projects the Institute and its broad development community had created, and I felt a need to share it in order to get "Vygotsky the developmentalist" into the conversations and debates taking place. Originally published in 2009 and republished with additional chapters in 2016, *Vygotsky at Work and Play* was my attempt at weaving together my personal experience of Vygotskian-inspired projects (in psychotherapy, schooling, youth development, workplace development, and police–community relations) and articulating the unique performance-based methodology of development and learning and its roots in Vygotsky's work.

Development, Learning, and Impediments to Them

Throughout this book, I have described and tried to show human development as an activity—not an unfolding—and as a social, relational activity—not an individual accomplishment. People are capable of engaging in lifelong, continuous development. If you want to learn more about the methodological and political problems psychologists see with the traditional stage-like understanding of development, there are two books written in the 1990s that, in my view, are still the best at exposing the biases of developmental psychology and how they are impediments to social justice.

Development—Not Pure and Not Simple

Deconstructing Developmental Psychology

Written in 1994, *Deconstructing Developmental Psychology*, by Erica Burman, shows how mainstream developmental psychology normalizes childhood and, in the process, pathologizes children and their families, especially mothers, who are other than middle class and white. Updated with a new edition in 2016, the book addresses children's rights, child protection, and other issues in which current policies involving children are shaped by mainstream psychology's ideas of development.

Growing Critical: Alternatives to Developmental Psychology

John Morss's 1996 book presents a painstaking, yet accessible, history and analysis of ways that Marxism, psychoanalysis, post-structuralism, and feminism have been offering challenges to developmental psychology since the 1970s. I learned a lot from this book when I first read it. I remember reading with delight and wonder Morss's conclusion that development does not exist—and I, a developmentalist, agreed with him! You have to read his book to discover how that can be. If you do, read the updated 2023 edition.

Let's Develop!

In addition to being an apt slogan for a developmentalist, this phrase is the title of a book by the late Fred Newman, co-founder of the institute and my longtime colleague (full title: *Let's Develop! A Guide to Continuous Personal Growth*). Newman weaves philosophical and methodological challenges to the assumptions we carry around with us with dozens of scenarios drawn from the daily lives of his clients. He urges us, through illustration, to avoid getting to the bottom of things and, instead, to seek our cure to what ails us through developing. Widely read by teens and adults, *Let's Develop!* has been translated into Chinese and Serbian.

Podcasts

I sometimes like to listen to a podcast instead of or before I read an author's book. If this applies to you, I invite you to listen to these podcasts I have done recently. Each interviewer approached the topic of development from a different angle, and I responded accordingly.

- "The Radical Therapist." Chris Hoff, host of "The Radical Therapist" podcast series (2015–), invited me to explore the history and development of social therapeutics, the dualisms and dichotomies that run rampant in psychology, and "The Developmentalist" project (episode #108; Hoff, 2022).
- "Rebel, Reject, Create." I jumped at the chance to respond to "What is a developmentalist?" when I spoke with David Chislett, host and creator of the podcast, "Rebel, Reject, Create." (https://medium.com/an-idea/be-the-change-rebel-reject-create-1035317af389)
- "Engaging Presence." I really enjoyed my conversation with Sally Fox on her podcast, "Engaging Presence," where we meandered through play, performance, and development (Fox, 2023).
- "Laugh Box." And what fun it was to speak with Katy Bee and Jim-Bob, hosts of the "Laugh Box" (podcast of the Association for Applied and Therapeutic Humor; Williams and Bee, 2017–). I didn't expect to, but I talked about how I'm developing! (https://laughbox.aath.org/e/episode-95-aath-interviews-dr-lois-holzman-co-founder-of-the-east-side-institute/)

Learning = Knowing (and Language Is an Activity)

My focus on continuous development, in theory and in practice, is a challenge to the ways in which people, from quite an early age, are culturally shaped to overvalue knowing and knowledge. Clients come to us wanting to know, usually wanting to know what's wrong with them and what to do. Teachers and students go to school expecting to be judged as knowers. I already mentioned *The Overweight Brain*, but, if you would like to learn more about the dangers of knowing and the values of non-knowing growing (developing), here are a few sources.

Schools for Growth: Radical Alternatives to Current Educations Models

If you wonder how it came to be that schools in the US fail to educate so many young people, I invite you to pick up this book (Holzman, 1997b). I first explore the Vygotskian inspiration for my critique of school's overemphasis on individual cognitive skills and go on to present case studies that illustrate how three different approaches to democratic and developmental education leave knowing outside the classroom door and focus, instead, on creating environments for imaginations, sociability, and responsibility to flourish and lead the learning journeys.

"Build a School in the Cloud"

This is a prize-winning TED Talk in which Sugata Mitra presents his "Hole in the Wall" experiment with children in Delhi's Kalkaji slum and one computer. Since then, he has continued to conduct educational research with new technologies and teach widely, sharing his conviction and evidence from many countries and situations that, in the absence of supervision and formal teaching, children can teach themselves and each other—if they're motivated by curiosity. I urge you to watch it. And, while you're at it, I invite you to listen in/watch Mitra and me in conversation exploring the end of knowing. In 2019, I sat down (virtually) with Mitra for a lively conversation exploring the end of knowing (East Side Institute, 2019, https://vimeo.com/554413963).

Pedagogy of the Oppressed

Paolo Freire wrote this book more than a half a century ago (1970), but it is timeless. It is critical pedagogy in the best sense of that term. Based in large part on his experiences teaching peasants in Chile, Freire argues for an emancipatory education that can liberate the poor from the fear and passivity that stem from their oppression in order that they can fight to regain their humanity. His description of schooling as the banking model of education and of dialogue as liberating us inspires me today, as it did decades ago on first reading.

Teaching to Transgress: Education as the Practice of Freedom

When writer, educator, social critic, feminist (the list goes on) bell hooks passed away in 2021, there was a flurry of tributes to this remarkable woman and a resurgence of interest in her life and work. I have no way of knowing if that resurgence continues, but I certainly hope so. I recommend anything she wrote, but, if it's education and schools that have your interest at the moment, *Teaching to Transgress* should be first on your list. Written in 1994, in this book of personal narrative and broad cultural commentary as a Black woman, what hooks passionately advocates for resonates strongly with the developmentalist's insistence on relationality and relating to people "a head taller"—especially, but not only, as a counterforce to a racist culture.

Wittgenstein's Writings

Fred Newman and I had hundreds of conversations about language. His background was the philosophy of language, and mine was the psychology of language and the field of linguistics. At the beginning, it was almost like we were using two different languages to talk about language! But we agreed that there was something important in these two approaches that had to do with what and how people learn and develop and, equally, how people understand learning and developing. As we came to understand and appreciate each other's traditions, we discovered not only compatibility but also the opportunity to create something new through synthesis. Newman introduced me to Wittgenstein, and I introduced him to Vygotsky—and we "introduced" them to each other. We wrote about how we synthesized them in several of the books mentioned elsewhere (e.g., *Unscientific Psychology*, *Lev Vygotsky: Revolutionary Scientist*, *The Overweight Brain*).

I invite you to dip into Wittgenstein himself—a brilliant philosopher and deeply moral (and morally tortured) human being whose writings are very challenging—he writes in numbered paragraphs, often as dialogue with an imaginary person. I find them completely enjoyable. Try these two books and see what you think: *Philosophical Investigations* (1953) and *The Blue and Brown Books* (1965).

Play and Performance

Homo Ludens: A Study of the Play-Element in Culture

Johan Hoizinga was a Dutch cultural historian during the Nazis' rise to power (of which he was critical). His 1938 book, *Homo Ludens*, was published in English in 1949 and has become an international classic, which is why I recommend it. He presents play as the key activity in flourishing societies and cultures and traces the "playful human" from the time of Plato, through the Middle Ages and the Renaissance, up to modern civilizations of the 20th century.

"Play Helps Us Grow at Any Age"

What a challenge it was to prepare and perform a TED Talk! "Play Helps Us Grow at Any Age" was my first (and likely my last) such performance. Figuring out what to say and how to say it in 14 minutes and then memorizing it and rehearsing it was so very challenging. Like running a marathon, it's definitely worth doing once! (I've actually run three marathons, but I decided that was enough.) You can watch the talk, presented at TEDx Navesink in 2014, and see if I have convinced you to become a fellow play revolutionary (or at least embrace play as a way to keep developing).

"The Decline of Play"

At that same TEDx Conference, Peter Gray presented "The Decline of Play." Gray is a lifelong passionate advocate for play, as both researcher and human being. In this talk, he presents a compelling argument linking the dramatic increases in restrictions on children's freedom to play and equally dramatic increase in anxiety, depression, feelings of helplessness, suicide, and narcissism in children and adolescents. "The Decline of Play" has been viewed over 78,000 times. I invite you to join those thousands and watch it.

Performance of a Lifetime: A Practical-Philosophical Guide to the Joyous Life

Fred Newman followed his *Let's Develop!* with a most unusual self-help book—one that offers no simple lessons and makes no unrealistic claims (Newman, 1996). Instead, Newman shows how to live a joyous life through performing philosophy. For him, one of the things this involves is embracing both the banality and majesty of human endeavor. What he means by joyous, by performing, and by philosophy will definitely surprise you. I greatly admire Newman's performance in this book.

Performance Breakthrough: A Radical Approach to Success at Work

Ditto Cathy Salit, author of *Performance Breakthrough*, in which she offers up the tools of performance to coaches and business consultants.

Salit wrote this book based on her 20-year performance as a workshop designer and leader and coach to executives and managers at some of the most successful global firms. Salit is a longtime colleague of mine and excellent "student" of developmentalist methodology. One of the delights of this book, for me, is to experience the creative reworking and reframing of the philosophical-performatory practice that has been my life's work. With what she calls "the becoming principle," Salit has made it her own.

Performance Activism: Precursors and Contemporary Pioneers

If you recall from Chapter 14, one of ways social therapeutics spread was through the conferences we hosted under the name Performing the World. So many people in so many different cultures and nation-states were experimenting with various kinds of performance. And so many of them were community and/or political activists, putting existing performance tools to work and inventing new ones in the name of social and cultural transformation. If you are curious—about whether performance is or could be a new form of resistance, about how and when and where performance began to be used this way, and about the people doing the work on the ground to bring a movement into existence—I invite you to read Dan Friedman's *Performance Activism* (2021).

"All Power to the Developing"

The institute launched a podcast, "All Power to the Developing," in 2021 to give as many of these performance activists as we could a platform (Wandan, 2021–). You probably realize by now that there is great overlap between performance activists and developmentalists. This podcast gives both a much-needed stage to tell their stories. As of this writing, 52 episodes have been produced and are available on all major podcast sites. A few times a week, I listen to one while on a walk. I invite you to join me.

Performative Research

If you have an interest in research, you might want to check out these resources on the emerging field known as performative social science. I first encountered it (before it had a name) through my own work.

Playing with Purpose: Adventures in Performative Social Science

In my courses as a faculty member during the 1980s–90s at Empire State College, SUNY, I played around with having students perform their understanding of course readings and their research projects. This was before these kinds of teaching innovations had a name. The first book on the subject that I recall is *Playing with Purpose: Adventures in Performative Social Science*, by Ken Gergen and Mary Gergen, which they wrote back in 2012. It explores the origins of performative social science, makes a strong case for enriching the social sciences through performative work, and contains many of their own performance pieces.

Doing Performative Social Science: Creativity in Doing Research and Reaching Communities

This is a more recent and more comprehensive book than *Playing with Purpose*. *Doing Performative Social Science* is a volume edited by Kip Jones (2022). The contributing authors provide an array of examples of supplementing or replacing traditional methods of research and presentation with tools from the arts, including photography, dance, drama, filmmaking, poetry, and fiction. I especially enjoy presentations of research finds presented through performance.

"Dance Your Ph.D."

Yes, you really can. There's even a contest for the best. I've enjoyed several of them—and learned a lot about science in the process. Check out the videos from "Dance Your Ph.D." (www.science.org/content/page/dance-your-ph-d)

Critiques and Alternatives to Mainstream Psychology

The calls for a psychology that takes into account the complexity and totality of humans as social-cultural-historical beings go back at least as far as the 19th century. Vygotsky's entire enterprise, beginning with his "search for method" (discussed in Chapter 14), was one of the first that I encountered, but by no means was it the last. Skeptical of the dualistic and causal assumptions of the psychology I was encountering in graduate school, I familiarized myself with as many types of critiques as I could, from the scientific to the philosophical to the political. I delved deepest, and continue to do so, into the works of critical and postmodern psychologists. Among the most numerous of those who have identified as postmodern are social constructionists. Below you will find some of the works I recommend, some for their wide scope and others for their therapeutic depth. The widest scope is found in the following three reference books.

Handbook of Critical Psychology

Critical psychologists are concerned with power and the ways in which mainstream psychology's practices and norms uphold the status quo, hinder social justice, and maintain the oppression of specific groups. I am concerned with these issues also and, in that way, I am a critical psychologist. In another way, however, I am not. The many critical perspectives that fall under this rubric can be categorized as ideologically based (for example, Marxist psychology), identity-based (for example, psychology of women, Black psychology), or epistemologically based (indigenous psychologies). I do not think that being a developmentalist puts me in any of these categories. However, I value highly the work of critical psychologists and the ways their thinking has influenced not only the practices of my colleagues and me but (ever so slowly) the fields of psychology and psychotherapy. I invite you to dip your toes into it.

The best way is I know is with the *Handbook of Critical Psychology* (2015), which provides a great overview of a perspective in and on psychology that gets far too little attention. The volume was edited by Ian Parker, perhaps the most widely known critical psychologist. Parker has written dozens of books (all worth a read) and, importantly, edited at least a dozen more that include non-western critical and alternative voices.

Palgrave Encyclopedia of Critical Perspectives on Mental Health

Recognizing the interdisciplinarity of the mental health field, this volume looks across national borders and areas of research and practice to present critical perspectives from psychology, psychiatry, sociology, education, and medicine (Lester and O'Reilly, 2021). It's another excellent way to learn more about critical psychology and new understandings of mental health.

Sage Handbook of Social Constructionist Practice

I am a social constructionist myself and so I was honored to be included in this book (McNamee et al., 2020; my chapter, "Constructing Social Therapeutics," is mentioned above). I especially like that it showcases the range and variations in the multilevel social constructionist tradition from many fields, including organizational development, therapy, health care, education, research, and community building.

If you do some research on or come across the term social constructionism, you will quickly be introduced to Ken Gergen. His work is known and studied worldwide. He was a social constructionist before there was such a thing, and many credit him with founding social constructionism. I invite you to pick up any of his dozens of books and become engrossed in a kind of studied passion for involving people in transforming social life into ways of living that are consistent with and celebrate our relationality. Two of my favorites are *The Saturated Self: Dilemmas of Identity in Contemporary Life* (that shouldn't surprise you) (2000), and *Realities and Relationships: Soundings in Social Construction* (1994).

If you like to delve into origins, I invite you to look at two books published way back in 1992. I read them in the 1990s and was excited to realize I and my colleagues were not alone.

Therapy as Social Construction, edited by Gergen and his longtime colleague Sheila McNamee (1992), includes essays by a dozen theorists and practitioners. As a whole, the book argues for the rejection of the therapist as an expert and emphasizes the process and mutually enriching and developmental elements inherent in a trusting therapeutic interaction.

Psychology and Postmodernism, edited by Steiner Kvale (1992), is considered to be the first book to explore the implications of postmodernist ideas for psychology. Relevant postmodern concerns—the nature of the self, locally situated rather than universal knowledge, and the pivotal role of language in social life—are examined for their implications for what psychology could become.

Bringing Alternatives Together

Postmodern Psychologies, Societal Practice, and Political Life

Postmodern Psychologies, Societal Practice, and Political Life is a book I edited with John Morss (the author of *Growing Critical*, mentioned above). It draws on presentations at a conference, "Unscientific Psychology: Conversations with Other Voices," that I organized in 1997. This international event brought together in dialogue, for the first time, the two camps of critical psychology and postmodern psychology proponents. It was also the first time a conference featuring academics was explicitly performance-based, with audience and presenters creating performances as an innovative (and risky!) way to continue conversations on the academic presentations. For these two firsts, I think of the conference and book as a turning point in my development as a developmentalist.

Unscientific Psychology

Unscientific psychology continued to be explored with a book Fred Newman and I co-authored, entitled *Unscientific Psychology: A Cultural-Performatory Approach to Understanding Human Life* (1996/2006). The book is a bit of a scholarly rant against the institution, the methods and conceptions, and the practices of institutionalized psychology. After delineating the problematic philosophical underpinnings of the discipline of psychology (which we call a pseudoscience), we detail the origins and assumptions of what we call psychology's myths—the individual, mental illness, and development. The book ends with chapters on the development community and its creating a cultural-performatory approach to being human. If you like polemics (and want to learn some shocking history), give this book a read.

Challenging Diagnosis

In Chapter 14, I referred to the controversy surrounding the publication of the fifth edition of the *Diagnostic and Statistical Manual of Mental Disorders* (*DSM-5*) and diagnosis more broadly. If you are required to diagnose in your mental health or educational practice, or if you or a friend or family member has been given a diagnosis, I urge you to check out these valuable resources.

From 2017 to 2019, the American Psychological Association devoted five issues of its *Journal of Humanistic Psychology* to a Special Issue Series on "Diagnostic Alternatives." The articles in these issues are indispensable. The same journal also published an article reporting on what people think of diagnosis, entitled "Diagnosis: A thousand people speak out," based on a survey that the institute carried out at street fairs and online (Holzman and Genn, 2019).

> Mad in America (MIA) is a non-profit organization that serves as a catalyst for rethinking psychiatric care in the United States (and abroad). We believe that the current drug-based paradigm of care has failed our society, and that scientific research, as well as the lived experience of those who have been diagnosed with a psychiatric disorder, calls for profound change. (www.madinamerica. com/mission-statement/)

This online resource has a webzine updated daily with news and essays, continuing education offerings, and an MIA Radio podcast series. In addition to the Americas, there are MIAs in nine other countries. (You can read my columns on MIA at www.madinamerica.com/author/lois/).

A Disorder 4 Everyone (AD4E) is another online resource that hosts events that challenge the dominant diagnostic culture in mental health.

I mentioned above "The Radical Therapist" as a podcast I was a guest on. It is a wonderful series that I cannot recommend too highly. Some of host Chris Hoff's guests speak of diagnosis, but the show is much broader as it explores "the intersections of collaborative therapy, psychology, philosophy, art, and science & technology." There are well over a hundred half-hour conversations you can listen to and be enlightened. I certainly have.

I don't think the work "diagnosis" appears in Irshad Manji's *Don't Label Me: An Incredible Conversation for Divided Times*. Yet, this book—on diversity, bigotry, and our common humanity—can easily be read as a searing indictment of diagnostic labeling. I love this book for its hard-hitting message, its convincing arguments, its two protagonists (the author and her dog), and its humor. I urge you to read it. I had the privilege of sitting down with Manji for a public conversation. If you'd like to hear it, go to the institute's Vimeo channel (https://vimeo.com/esinstitute) and scroll down to "Labels, Learning and Love" (Manji and Holzman, 2019).

Still Wondering?

I hope you found this chapter worthwhile. I wrote it hoping to create some new curiosities and new pathways for you to explore, should you want to. It was quite challenging. Acknowledging my lack of breadth, I was keenly aware of so many valuable resources I was leaving out and equally aware that some readers might be offended by this or that omission. I had to remind myself many times that my goal was not to put together a comprehensive annotated bibliography, but to give you more of what shaped me as a developmentalist. It was, as I said, challenging, and it was also sometimes surprising and ultimately rewarding. And so, I invite you to create your own narrative of what shaped you.

BIBLIOGRAPHY

American Psychiatric Association. (2022). *Diagnostic and statistical manual of mental disorders, text revision DSM-5-tr*. American Psychiatric Association.

Burman, E. (1994/2016). *Deconstructing developmental psychology*. Routledge.

Chislett, D. (2023). Host, Rebel, Reject, Create podcast. Lois Holzman, *The Developmentalist*. May 10, 2023. https://davidchislett.com/podcast/

Cole, M., Hood, L., & McDermott, R. (1994). *Ecological niche picking: Ecological invalidity as an axiom of experimental cognitive psychology*. LCHC and ICHD, Rockefeller University.

East Side Institute. (2019). An exploration of the end of knowing: A webinar with Sugata Mitra and Lois Holzman. https://eastsideinstitute.org/wp-content/uploads/2019/07/Sugata-Mitra-Lois-Holzman_-The-End-of-Knowing-JW-copy.pdf

Ekman, P., & Friesen, W.V. (1971). Constants across cultures in the face and emotion. *Journal of Personality and Social Psychology, 17*(2), 124.

Freire, P. (1970). *Pedagogy of the oppressed*. Herder & Herder.

Fox, S. (2023). Host, Engaging Presence podcast. Lois Holzman, The art of becoming through play and performance. January 26, 2023. www.engagingpresence.com/lois-holzman-the-art-of-becoming-through-play-and-performance/

Friedman, D. (2021). *Performance activism: Precursors and contemporary pioneers*. Springer Nature.

Gergen, K.J. (1994). *Realities and relationships: Soundings in social construction*. Harvard University Press.

Gergen, K.J. (2000). *The saturated self: Dilemmas of identity in contemporary life*. Basic Books.

Gergen, K.J. (2001). *Social construction in context*. London: Sage.

Gergen, M., & Gergen, K.J. (2012). *Playing with purpose: Adventures in performative social science*. Routledge.

Gray, P. (2014). The decline of play. Presented at TEDx Navisink. www.youtube.com/watch?v=Bg-GEzM7iTk

Henig, R. (2004). Sorry, your eating disorder doesn't meet our criteria. *The New York Times*, November 4, 2004. www.nytimes.com/2004/11/30/health/psychology/sorry-your-eating-disorder-doesnt-meet-our-criteria.html

Hoff, C. (2015–). Host, The Radical Therapist podcast. https://chrishoffmft.podbean.com

Hoff, C. (2022). Host, The Radical Therapist podcast. Lois Holzman, Something other than psychology. Episode 108, November 22, 2022. https://chrishoffmft.podbean.com/e/the-radical-therapist-108--something-other-than-psychology-w-dr-lois-holzman/

Hoizinga, J. (1949). *Homo ludens: A study of the play-element of culture*. Routledge.

Holzman, L. (1997a). Developmental stage. *Special Children*, June/July, 32–35.

Holzman, L. (1997b). *Schools for growth: Radical alternatives to current educational models*. Routledge.

Holzman, L. (2004). Do boundaries inhibit the growth of new psychologies? 112th Convention of the American Psychological Association. Honolulu, Hawaii.

Holzman, L. (2009/2016). *Vygotsky at work and play*. Routledge.

Holzman, L. (2014a). Practicing method: Social therapy as practical–critical psychology. *Psychotherapy and Politics International*, *12*(3), 176–184. DOI:10.1002/ppi.1334.

Holzman, L. (2014b). Play helps us grow at any age. Presented at TEDx Navisink. www.youtube.com/watch?v=E4sdVE0Q9Lk

Holzman, L. (2015). Social therapy and creating an activist life. Presentation at conference on Healing Society at Fu Jen Catholic University, Taipei, Taiwan, April.

Holzman, L. (2016). The development community and its activist psychology. In R. House, D. Kalisch, & J. Maidman (Eds.), *The future of humanistic psychology*. PCCS.

Holzman, L. (2018a). *The overweight brain: How our obsession with knowing keeps us from getting smart enough to make a better world*. East Side Institute Press.

Holzman, L. (2018b). Zones of proximal development: Mundane and magical. In *The Routledge handbook of sociocultural theory and second language development*. Routledge, pp. 42–55.

Holzman, L. (2020a). Constructing social therapeutics. In S. McNamee, M.M. Gergen, C. Camargo-Borges, & E.F. Rasera (Eds.), *The Sage handbook of social constructionist practice*. *Sage*, pp. 171–182.

Holzman, L. (2020b). Vygotsky on the margins. In A.T. Neto, F. Liberali, & M. Dafermos (Eds.), *Revisiting Vygotsky for social change: Bringing together theory and practice*. Peter Lang, pp. 111–124.

Holzman, L., & Genn, E. (2019). Diagnosis: A thousand people speak out. *Journal of Humanistic Psychology*, *59*(1), 48–68.

Holzman, L., & Mendez, R. (2003). *Psychological investigations: A clinician's guide to social therapy*. Brunner-Routledge.

Holzman, L., & Morss, J. (2000). *Postmodern psychologies, societal practice, and political life*. Routledge.

Holzman, L., & Newman, F. (2012). Activity and performance (and their discourses) in social therapeutic practice. In A. Lock & T. Strong (Eds.), *Discursive perspectives in therapeutic practice*. Oxford University Press, pp. 184–195.

Holzman, L., & Newman, F., with Strong, T. (2004). Power, authority and pointless activity: The developmental discourse of social therapy. In T. Strong & D. Paré (Eds.), *Furthering talk: Advances in discursive therapies*. Springer Nature, pp. 73–86.

Hood, L., & McDermott, R. (1980). "Let's try to make it a good day"—some not so simple ways. *Discourse Processes, 3*(2), 155–168.

hooks, b. (1994). *Teaching to transgress.* Routledge.

Jones, K. (Ed.). (2022). *Doing performative social science: Creativity in doing research and reaching communities.* Taylor & Francis.

Kohlberg, L. (1973). Stages and aging in moral development—some speculations. *The Gerontologist, 13*(4), pp. 497–502. https://doi.org/10.1093/geront/13.4.497

Kvale, S. (Ed.). (1992). *Psychology and postmodernism.* Sage.

Lester, J.M., & O'Reilly, N. (Eds.). (2021). *The Palgrave encyclopedia of critical perspectives on mental health.* Cham: Springer International. https://link.springer.com/referencework/10.1007/978-3-030-12852-4#affiliations

Lock, A., & Strong, T. (Eds.). (2012). *Discursive perspectives in therapeutic practice.* Oxford University Press.

Lowe, V. (2008). Lev Vygotsky: One man's legacy through his life and theory. www.youtube.com/watch?v=tqjmQ6ts4SA

McNamee, S., & Gergen, K.J. (1992). *Therapy as social construction.* Sage.

McNamee, S., Gergen, M.M., Gergen, M., Camargo-Borges, C., & Rasera, E.F. (Eds.). (2020). The Sage handbook of social constructionist practice. Sage.

Manji, I. (2019). *Don't label me: An incredible conversation for divided times.* St. Martin's Press.

Manji, I., & Holzman, L. (2019). Labels, learning and love. Presentation, East Side Institute. https://vimeo.com/377574068

Maslow, A.H. (1958). A dynamic theory of human motivation. In C.L. Stacey & M. DeMartino (Eds.), *Understanding human motivation.* Howard Allen, pp. 26–47. https://doi.org/10.1037/11305-004

Mitra, S. (2013). Build a school in the cloud. TED prize presentation. www.ted.com/talks/sugata_mitra_build_a_school_in_the_cloud?subtitle=en

Morss, J.R. (1996/2023). *Growing critical: Alternatives to developmental psychology.* Routledge.

Neto, A.T., Liberali, F., & Dafermos, M. (2020). *Revisiting Vygotsky for social change: Bringing together theory and practice.* Peter Lang.

Newman, F. (1994). *Let's develop! A guide to continuous personal growth.* Castillo International.

Newman, F. (1996). *Performance of a lifetime: A practical-philosophical guide to the joyous life.* Castillo International.

Newman, F., & Holzman, L. (1993/2013). *Lev Vygotsky: Revolutionary scientist.* Routledge.

Newman, F., & Holzman, L. (1996/2006). *Unscientific psychology: A cultural-performatory approach to understanding human life.* IUniverse.

Parker, I. (Ed.). (2015). *Handbook of critical psychology.* Routledge.

Pernecky, T., & Holzman, L. (2019). Knowledge as play: Centering on what matters. In T. Pernecky (Ed.), *Postdisciplinary knowledge.* Routledge, Chapter 6. www.routledge.com/Postdisciplinary-Knowledge/Pernecky/p/book/9780429058561

Sackett, C., & Dabby, M. (2023). *Social therapeutic coaching: A practical guide to group and couples work.* Taylor & Francis.

Salit, C.R. (2016). *Performance breakthrough: A radical approach to success at work.* Hachette UK.

Singh, J.S. (2011). The vanishing diagnosis of Asperger's disorder. In *Sociology of Diagnosis,* Vol. 12. Emerald Group, pp. 235–257.

Shotter, J. (1991). Wittgenstein and psychology: On our "hook up" to reality. In A. Phillips-Griffiths (Ed.), *Wittgenstein: Centenary essays.* Cambridge: Cambridge University Press, pp.193–208.

Shotter, J. (1993a). *Conversational realities: Studies in social constructionism.* London: Sage.

Shotter, J. (1993b). *Cultural politics of everyday life: Social constructionism, rhetoric and knowing of the third kind.* Toronto: University of Toronto Press.

Van der Veer, R., & Valsiner, J. (Eds.). (1994). *The Vygotsky reader.* Blackwell.

Vygotsky, L.S. (1978). *Mind in society.* Harvard.

Vygotsky, L.S. (1987). *The collected works of L. S. Vygotsky. Volume 1.* Plenum.

Vygotsky, L.S. (1993). *The collected works of L. S. Vygotsky, Volumn 2, The fundamentals of defectology.* Plenum.

Vygotsky, L.S. (1994). The problem of the environment. In R. van der Veer & J. Valsiner (Eds.), *The Vygotsky reader.* Blackwell, pp. 338–354.

Vygotsky, L.S. (1997). *The collected works of L. S. Vygotsky, Volume 4, The history of the development of higher mental functions.* Springer.

Vygotsky, L.S. (1997). The historical meaning of the crisis in psychology: A methodological investigation. In *The collected works of L. S. Vygotsky, Volume 3.* Plenum, pp. 233–343.

Vygotsky, L.S. (1998). *The collected works of L. S. Vygotsky, Volume 5, Child psychology.* Springer.

Vygotsky, L.S. (2004). The collective as a factor in the development of the abnormal child. In R.W. Rieber & D.K. Robinson (Eds.), *The essential Vygotsky.* Kluwer Academic/Plenum, pp. 201–219.

Wandan, D. (2021–). Host, All Power to the Developing podcast. https://eastsideinstitute.org/resources/multimedia/podcasts/all-power-to-the-developing-podcast/

Williams, J-B., & Bee, K. (2017–). Hosts, Laugh Box, a podcast of the Association for Applied Therapeutic Humor.

Wittgenstein, L. (1953). *Philosophical investigations.* Blackwell.

Wittgenstein, L. (1965). *The blue and brown books.* Harper Torchbooks.

For Product Safety Concerns and Information please contact our EU
representative GPSR@taylorandfrancis.com
Taylor & Francis Verlag GmbH, Kaufingerstraße 24, 80331 München, Germany